On Architecture

Studies in Austrian Literature, Culture, and Thought

Adolf Loos

On Architecture

Selected and Introduced by
Adolf and Daniel Opel

Translated by Michael Mitchell

ARIADNE PRESS
Riverside, California

Translated from the German
Über Architektur
© 1995 Georg Prachner Verlag Wien

Library of Congress Cataloging-in-Publication Data

Loos, Adolf, 1870-1933
    [Über Architektur. English]
    On architecture / Adolf Loos ; selected and introduced by Adolf
and Daniel Opel ; translated by Michael Mitchell.
        p. cm. -- (Studies in Austrian literature, culture,
    and thought)
    Companion v. to: Ornament and crime. ©1998.
    ISBN 1-57241-098-1
        1. Architecture, Modern--19th century. 2. Architecture,
Modern--20th century. 3. Architecture--Austria--Vienna.
I. Opel, Adolf, 1935- II. Opel, Daniel. III. Loos, Adolf,
1870-1933. Ornament and crime. IV. Title. V. Series.

NA27.L6513 2002
720'.9--dc21
                                                    2001045094

Cover Design:
Art Director, Designer: George McGinnis

Copyright ©2002
by Ariadne Press
270 Goins Court
Riverside, CA 92507

SONDERPOSTMARKE
»125. GEBURTSTAG
VON ADOLF LOOS«

Entwurf von P. Sinawehl

*„Loos-Haus" am Michaelerplatz
in Wien (siehe Seite 93)*

Special Issue Postage Stamp
Commemorating the 125th Birthday of Adolf Loos
Design by P. Sinawehl
Loos-House on Michaelerplatz in Vienna (see page 92)

Contents

INTRODUCTION

"I would be extremely grateful if you could insert a notice in your esteemed newspaper to the effect that I am not identical with the Viennese architect who said, 'Ornament is a crime.' The suspicion that I did maintain such a thing is justified, as I gave a lecture, seventeen years ago, with the title 'Ornament and Crime,' in which I demonstrated the psychological connection between ornamentation (tattooing) and criminality." (Reader's letter to the *Neue Freie Presse*, Vienna, May 26, 1925)

This belated-sounding remark by the architect, Adolf Loos, on the theme of ornamentation and its elimination, which even today is inextricably bound up with his name, might strike those who know his work and have read his writings as somewhat paradoxical, to say the least. There are those for whom Loos is the "enemy of ornament" and nothing more. Had he changed his mind? Did he no longer want anything to do with all the things he had spent thirty years fighting for and against? The devotees of psychoanalysis might see it as a surprising conversion to the pleasure principle and proof of its ultimate primacy, given that for them Loos's theory of the repression of ornamentation is nothing other than a denial of the pleasure principle and all imaginative play. Others, finally, can interpret it as confirmation of the contradictions and inconsistencies they claim to have found in Loos since, as is well known, he did not leave a unified oeuvre, but articles scattered through journals and newspapers or originally conceived as lectures, all aimed at the general public.

Nikolaus Pevsner begins and ends his introduction to the English edition of Ludwig Münz and Gustav Künstler's monograph, *Adolf Loos — Pioneer of Modern Architecture*, with the statement, "Adolf Loos remains an enigma." And he called on the friends and students of Loos still living at the time — 1966 — to try and help solve the mystery. For Pevsner it was incomprehensible that, in the second decade of the twentieth century, such a radical thinker, because of his admiration for classical antiquity, should turn himself into the advocate of classicism in architecture and of classical ornamentation as an organizing factor, and give his design for the *Chicago Tribune* newspaper building the form of a Doric column. "Nobody can falsify himself. So the interpretation attempted in this introduction must be faulty or the evidence must be incomplete. For the time being at any rate the enigma remains." Heinrich Kulka, one of Loos's students who later worked with him, responded to Pevsner's call in his review of the book, partly printed in the journal *Architectural Design*, where he stresses that "Loos was no enigma, at least not for those who truly knew and understood him. His ideas were all of a piece and he was the essence of clarity. Loos made the principles of architectural creation plain."

To all those who have come to know Loos and his work — which does appear to be inherently paradoxical — the letter with which we opened our introduction will be one more indication that Loos's ultimate concern was more comprehensive and that his repeated criticism of the waste of labor and material in producing ornamentation was only one partial aspect of his argument. It seems most likely that what Loos was seeking to distance himself from was the *cliché* which the — often imprecise — linking of the concepts of "ornament" and "crime" had become in the time since he first formulated it, the "cliché as intellectual (and linguistic) ornament," in the words of his comrade-in-arms, Karl Kraus.

Precisely when dealing with a phenomenon such as Adolf Loos it is essential to get away from this reductionist view, which is so widespread today. There is no doubt that he was one of the most evolutionary and far-sighted minds ever to be active in Austria and Central Europe; at the same time he was a great traditionalist who constantly appealed to classical antiquity. He himself was a "man who tamed untrammeled imagination," as he called Karl Friedrich Schinkel, the architect of Prussian classicism.

The assessment of his actual significance has changed over the years. As early as 1964 Münz and Künstler, in their monograph *Der Architekt Adolf Loos — Darstellung seines Schaffens in Werkgruppen*, saw the main focus of his work not as his struggle against ornamentation but as his great *positive* contributions, namely his spatial plan and his vision in urban development. The large-scale Loos exhibitions of recent years, which have allowed people to see, in the form of architectural models, the countless projects that never got off the drawing board, have made us aware of what our environment, above all the city of Vienna, would be like if they had all been carried out. "If Loos were allowed to do the interior design for the world, then things would be in the kind of state a person is in when he has a clear conscience." This comment by Alfred Polgar, in his address on the occasion of Loos's sixtieth birthday in 1930, was echoed more than fifty years later when Julius Posener, on the occasion of the opening of a Loos exhibition at the Berlin Academy of Arts in 1983, recalled the way classical antiquity was employed to instill in artists a sense of dignity as a counterweight to the excesses of both the Baroque and the *Sezession*, going on to point out that anyone who entered a house of the great educator, Adolf Loos, was entering not a palace but a middle-class environment — but one that had dignity.

Loos's educational side comes out repeatedly in his demand for economy. His "second great achievement," the *spatial plan* — solving the ground plan in three dimensions — also ultimately derives from his principle of economy: just as ornamentation produced by the craftsman means, according to Loos, a waste of material and labor — and is therefore a crime against workers' health and the nation's assets — so for him the waste of space means a waste of energy and efficiency for those who live in the house and therefore a reduction in their quality of life. Until now architects, he maintained, had been compelled to make the toilet as high as the dining room. Loos's spatial plan, on the other hand, is not determined by the height of each story and allocates a different height to each room according to need. "This invention of mine would have saved humanity much time and labor in its development," Loos wrote in his obituary for the cabinetmaker, Josef Veillich, in the *Frankfurter Zeitung* of March 21, 1929, continuing in a footnote, "That is the great revolution in architecture . . . Just as mankind will one day play chess in three dimensions, so other architects will find spatial solutions for the ground plan."

Economy as a principle of life, economy right down to routine everyday tasks, proves to be a constant factor in Loos's thirty years work as architect and writer. And a look at his life's work serves to confirm the conclusion that his struggle against ornamentation was only one stage along a road which he followed singlemindedly, a road marked out by ethical, social and aesthetic values. But it was a decisive and formative stage, and one which provided a leitmotiv for the architectural, cultural and intellectual history of the twentieth century.

One aim of the present selection, which gathers together the most important texts Adolf Loos wrote on his central topic of *architecture*, is to correct a one-sided and often reductionist view of his achievement. An essential complement to this is the volume that has already appeared, *Ornament and Crime: Selected Essays*, which contains all Loos's writings on the theme of ornament and related topics. It is not the purpose of these two books to analyse or interpret Loos's ideas and examine their relevance to what is actually happening in our twenty-first century, but rather to provide a starting point for such studies. For that reason Loos's articles have been translated here from the form in which they were originally published.

1896, the year he returned to Vienna after a three-year stay in the United States, saw the start of his critical preoccupation with the imperial capital which was to become a lifetime's work. Vienna seemed to him to be backward in every respect. Its architecture was dominated by historicism. It was also the time when *art nouveau* started to blossom: the founding of the Vienna *Sezession* came in the same year — 1897 — as his first reviews of exhibitions appeared, articles in which he always managed to turn the discussion of the specific topic into a declaration of principles.

His first known publications are in the Viennese journal, *Die Zeit*. In "A Competition Organized by the City of Vienna" he inveighs against the results of a competition for plans for an exhibition pavilion to be erected at the forthcoming Jubilee

Exhibition to celebrate the fiftieth anniversary of Emperor Franz Josef's accession. In his early writings Loos still supports the projects of Joseph Maria Olbrich and Josef Hoffmann, whose work he was later to condemn: "Looking at their work, every art lover must say to himself, if only the authorities would at least try! These projects are Viennese to the very core, Viennese in their effortless harmony of forms. The English details, to which, by the way, I *strongly object*, only affect superficial aspects." Nowhere else in his writings does Loos allow himself the slightest criticism of things taken over from the English-speaking world. Throughout his life he remained convinced of the absolute superiority of the English and American lifestyle. The formative influence of his years in America can be seen in many of his comments and judgments and in the frequency with which he refers to the World Exhibition in Chicago, which he visited. Beyond that, however, there is scarcely anything in his writings to provide clues for a biographer about his time in America.

There is a story that came from the Croatian architect, Viktor Kovacic — a friend of Loos in his early years who collaborated with him at the beginning of the 1920s on an entry for a competition to rebuild the Esplanade Hotel in Zagreb — that during his stay in America Loos came across the hand-made products of the Shakers, whose societies were so flourishing toward the end of the nineteenth century that they were represented at international exhibitions. Loos is even said to have learned brick-laying in a Shaker community, and it is certainly true that after his return to Austria he liked to emphasize that it was more important to him to be a time-served bricklayer than to have studied at the Technical University. There is still no evidence of direct contact between Loos and Shaker culture, but there are striking parallels.

As far as his work as a journalist was concerned, 1898 was the most fruitful year for Loos, who was still waiting for a large-scale architectural commission. It was the year Olbrich's *Sezession* building was erected and *Ver Sacrum* first appeared. The latter was the journal of the Vienna *Sezession*, and Loos was not above writing for it; at least at the time he was still in agreement with the *Sezession* in their rejection of historicism. Two articles of his appeared there: "To Our Young Architects" and "The Potemkin City." The latter, one of his best-known pieces, is his first unconditional declaration of war on Ringstraße Vienna with the sham, second-hand splendor of its façades.

In that same year "The Old and the New Style in Architecture" appeared. Written for a competition organized by the journal, *Der Architekt*, this essay, together with *Ornament and Crime* and *Architecture*, both of which were written ten years later, is one of Loos's significant programmatic statements of principle. Loos only won the second prize.

1898 was also the year of the Jubilee Exhibition in Vienna, and Loos was given the opportunity of writing a whole series of articles on this international event for the most prestigious national newspaper, the *Neue Freie Presse*. With his weekly reports his name suddenly became known throughout the Austro-Hungarian monarchy and beyond. His unorthodox views and paradoxical manner of formulating them aroused a wave of enthusiastic agreement, but also vehement disagreement. The first article, "The Exhibition Buildings: The New Style," appeared on 8 May 1898, the day after the opening, and a slightly abridged version was printed shortly afterwards in the Munich journal *Dekorative Kunst* under the title "The Vienna Jubilee Exhibition." From then until the exhibition closed on 18 October Loos published a further eighteen reports in the *Neue Freie Presse*. Two of these — "Building Materials" and "The Principle of Cladding" — have been included in the present volume, since they deal specifically with questions of architecture. The others are contained in the volume *Ornament and Crime*, as they fit in more closely with the theme of that collection.

The first book on Adolf Loos, written by a journalist, Karl Marilaun, in 1922, contains a vivid description of his spectacular entry on the stage of European cultural history: "It was at the end of the nineties that his name was first heard. He had returned from America and preached American values in Vienna. He preached reason, authenticity, hygiene, time-saving, a decent lifestyle.

At that time — the *fin de siècle* — the arts and crafts in Vienna were geared to the very opposite of reason, authenticity, thrift, health and economy in all areas of life.

Adolf Loos was clearly no longer Viennese. He no longer had *heart*, he neglected neither principles nor punctuality, he was disagreeably humorless in serious matters. His response to America and to Europe was an unconditional yes, consequently he became the "man who said no" to everything here in Vienna.

That was the label Loos acquired, and he spent twenty years preaching the advantages of a European way of life to the Viennese shut away in their own little world on the banks of the Danube.

After the end of the series of articles on the Jubilee Exhibition Loos made only sporadic appearances in the pages of the *Neue Freie Presse*. In the years that followed he occasionally wrote for other newspapers and it was not until 1903 that he took up regular journalistic activity again — or at least planned to. With *Das Andere — ein Blatt zur Einführung abendländischer Kultur in Österreich: geschrieben von Adolf Loos* (The Other - A Magazine to Promote the Introduction of Western Culture in Austria: Written by Adolf Loos) he attempted to create a vehicle for his own views, unencumbered by editorial interference. The first number appeared as a supplement to *Kunst — Halbmonatszeitschrift für Kunst und alles andere* (Art — a Bimonthly Periodical for Art and Everything Else), edited by Peter Altenberg; the second, and last, as an independent journal. Loos collected material for a third volume of *Das Andere*, but it was never published.

Toward the end of 1903 Loos received his first big commission: the *Villa Karma* near Montreux on Lake Geneva with which he was fully occupied over the next few years. Despite that, he pursued the idea of publishing another journal, which was to have the title: *Das Leben — ein Blatt zur Einführung abendländischer Kultur in Österreich* (Life — a Magazine to

Promote the Introduction of Western Culture in Austria). In a notice about it in the Berlin literary magazine, *Die Zukunft,* he wrote that he only intended to stay in charge of it himself for a year, explaining, "My profession — I am an architect — does not permit me to devote myself for years on end to such a strenuous sideline as writing a periodical. The purpose of the magazine will be to make my main profession easier. I design interiors. I can only do that for people of Western Culture. I had the good fortune to spend three years in America where I got to know the forms of Western Culture. Since I am convinced of their superiority, it would show a lack of principle to descend to the Austrian level. That leads to struggles, struggles in which I stand alone. The aristocracy — until now the only importer of the Western way of life — has lost all influence since the state and those in charge of education have capitulated to a school of thought which does not create forms from a way of life, but wants to create a way of life from forms. It was made difficult for ordinary people to acquire Western Culture because a wall was erected between the aristocracy and the people: The *Sezession.* The purpose of my magazine is to make breaches in that wall."

In 1904 Loos published two more essays in Maximilian Harden's *Die Zukunft,* "Der Sattlermeister" (The Master Saddler), a reprint from the second number of *Das Andere)* and "Keramika" (Pottery), probably intended for the new magazine he planned but which never came to fruition. Under the title "Vom Gehen, Stehen, Sitzen, Liegen, Schlafen, Essen, Trinken" (On Walking, Standing, Sitting, Lying, Sleeping, Eating and Drinking) this latter formed the basis of one of Loos's most provocative lectures, and an abridged version appeared in Herwarth Walden's *Der Sturm* in 1911.

In a second phase of journalistic activity around 1908 Loos wrote what were to become some of his best-known texts. Following his attendance at the convention in Munich of the German *Werkbund,* which had been founded the previous year, he wrote a violent attack on the organization which appeared in *März. Halbmonatsschrift für deutsche Kultur:* "Die Überflüssigen"

(Surplus to Requirements). The editor took the precaution of following the article with a note justifying the decision to print it: "Since Adolf Loos, the Viennese 'architect and writer, artist and thinker' as Meyer-Graefe calls him, will only be known to a small proportion of our readers, it seems appropriate to append a note on him so that our readers will not think he is some bullyboy hack whose sole purpose is to denigrate decent people such as the members of the *Werkbund*. Ten years ago Adolf Loos published in the *Neue Freie Presse* a series of articles on questions of interior decoration which attracted a great deal of attention, in particular exerting considerable influence on the development of 'applied' art in Vienna. Since then he has relinquished the word for the *deed* and has shown the way through his own 'interior designs.' His interior designs led to the development of a more severe, more serious style in Vienna and influenced Germany through the Viennese school. If he has now decided to take up the pen again, then it is certainly worth listening to what he has to say, and we are delighted to announce that he has promised *März* a series of short pieces on the subject of applied art and culture."

In the same year Loos wrote two of the promised articles, "Lob der Gegenwart" (In Praise of the Present) and "Kultur" (Culture). The *Werkbund* (whom Loos accused of German "junkerism" in production, trying to impose its will on the world) was given the opportunity of a reply in *März*, of which they took full advantage: ". . . Herr Loos praises the nineteenth century for 'the great achievement of clearly separating art from craft,' as if the defining element of an old piece of furniture were the allegorical representations, which we perhaps find superfluous, and not the simple form, which is linked to the whole world of art."

Does art for the *Werkbund* really mean inkwells with nymphs disporting themselves round the sides or manuals of anatomy with dissections of Greek statues? Such a suggestion is an insult to the artists attached to the *Werkbund*. — If Herr Loos had taken the trouble to read even a short report on the meeting in Munich he would surely have realized that what the association is aiming at is the exact opposite: we want to bring back decent craftwork through good training of apprentices and all other possible means. Beyond craftwork, we want to replace the trash with which the nation is currently plagued by 'quality work' in the broadest possible sense. In addition, the association brings together artists, craftsmen and manufacturers — not in order to create new sales opportunities for artists. But it is the artists who must support us with their advice and assistance, otherwise we won't get anywhere. Where should a wallpaper factory turn for beautiful patterns if not to the artist . . .?" This reply is signed by Walter Riezler, the same man who in 1924 edited the catalogue for the *Werkbund* exhibition, "Die Form ohne Ornament" (Form without Ornament), about which Loos, in the foreword to his collection of essays, *Trotzdem* (Nevertheless), commented angrily that this "perfidious book" managed both to ignore and to falsify his struggle; the responding echo, he said, believed itself to be the real voice.

The basic difference between the two standpoints is that Loos always argued for a scrupulous separation of art and craft, of art and industry. He was convinced that to give artists a determining role in design would mean attitudes to design and production would of necessity be influenced by the artists' subjective approach to work and their often inflated individualism. For Loos the *Werkbund* was merely a continuation of the endeavors of the *Sezession*. It was not from the inventors or destroyers of forms that Loos expected lasting innovations to emerge, but from the simple craftsman in his workshop and from his craft tradition, which had fostered and perfected the basic types of all objects of everyday use, tried and tested over many generations.

None of his writings and polemics has contributed so much to the Adolf Loos myth as his essay "Ornament und Verbrechen" (Ornament and Crime), which was also written in 1908. "It takes courage to awaken our sense of what is necessary," wrote Hermann Bahr, himself a tireless fighter for "modernism," in an article celebrating Loos on the occasion of his sixtieth birthday.

"There has never been a lack of willing souls to rouse us from our lethargy . . . but the victory belongs to Adolf Loos, for he supplied the cue for reflection on what we are and what we do: ORNAMENT AND CRIME. At that everyone paid heed, everyone repeated it. This piece has been translated into all languages. Who among us can boast of such widespread influence?"

Walter Benjamin has spoken of the "brilliant flash of lightning that ignited in that essay," which appeared in the *Frankfurter Zeitung* in 1908. Despite Benjamin's claim, however, the essay did not appear in the *Frankfurter Zeitung* until October 24, 1929, which is presumably the date of its first publication in German. A French version was printed in the Paris *Cahiers d'aujourd'hui* as early as June 1913. Loos also repeatedly presented "Ornament and Crime" as a public lecture. The first occasion was probably in Munich in September 1908; what is known for certain is that it was first given in Vienna on January 21, 1910. The *Fremden-Blatt* of the following day reported, "Under this extremely bizarre title the architect, Adolf Loos, yesterday gave a lecture under the auspices of the Academic Association for Literature and Music. At first sight the title seems rather pretentious, two concepts whose affinity is not immediately evident being coupled by a categorical 'and.' But with his succinct and persuasive forcefulness Adolf Loos managed to demonstrate their close relationship. He is an artist of great, mature culture, an artist of our own age, all of which came out vividly in a talk lasting scarcely half an hour. Adolf Loos is not a speaker in the ordinary sense of the word; his style lacks what one might call ornamentation, the incidental flourishes. His roots are in the aesthetic, his goal the monumental. The fanatical sincerity of this pugnacious man of conviction, which even his enemies would not dare to dispute, assures him an understanding response from his audience. The force of his well-formed sentences and clear arguments, the wit and intelligent strategy of his open attacks all give his lectures on art and culture a liveliness calculated to win over his hearers. . . . The speaker, who also touched on many topics of current interest, was rewarded with loud applause. The interesting lecture was followed by an often lively discussion which, however, in general confined itself to trivialities."

As many who heard him testify, Loos always spoke extempore, never read from a prepared text. In a festschrift for Loos's sixtieth birthday Max Thun-Hohenstein, the inventor of a revolutionary theory of motion, wrote, "He was the first person I heard who expressed his ideas freely, following an inner compulsion, and not only expressed his ideas freely in words, but also lived them out in front of his audience." Many of Loos's articles were originally conceived as lectures and a large number of his lectures were based on articles he had already written. There is a poster surviving for the repeat of the lecture, "Ornament and Crime," in Vienna in 1913 which was typeset according to Loos's instructions.

1910 was the year of the building with which Loos was to go down in the annals of the history of architecture: the "Loos building on Michaelerplatz," given the mocking nickname of the "building without eyebrows" by his enemies. It was the biggest commission he was ever to receive. In the years leading up to the First World War Loos was occupied on several further influential buildings and — since during his whole life he was never given an official teaching position — ran his own private school of building. During that period his journalistic work had to take a back seat, apart from the polemics concerning the Michaelerplatz building and some reflections on the principles of architecture, which Loos, with the exception of monuments and tombs, refused to consider an "art." Thus it seemed natural for the editors to gather all these writings together in one volume. *On Architecture* also contains notes taken by his students at Loos's school of building and the essays written in the 1920s on the social housing movement.

In the final year of the war and the immediate postwar years, when in what was now a tiny country there was hardly any work for architects and only the City of Vienna was left commissioning buildings, Loos once again spent more time on journalism. In the *Neues 8 Uhr-Blatt* he reported on exhibitions and the opening of the Technical Museum in Vienna, commented on questions of economics and the problem the new republican state was faced with in maintaining castles confiscated from the aristocracy. As he had already done in *Das Andere*, he answered readers' questions on fashion, etiquette and his constant theme of "art and craft."

In the following years Loos concerned himself mainly with urban development projects and — as chief architect of the City of Vienna's housing office — with the problem of creating social housing which also guaranteed a certain quality of life. His patent for "The House with One Wall" (1921) provides for a considerable saving in materials and labor in the erection of dwelling houses and commercial and industrial premises. It is a practical application developing logically out of his concept of economy.

In 1924, by which time a debate on the justification, or lack of it, of ornamentation already seemed an anachronism, he published his fundamental essay, "Ornament und Erziehung" (Ornament and Education), in *Wohnungskultur*, a journal from Brno, Czechoslovakia. The same number also contains the article "Von der Sparsamkeit" (On Thrift), which the editor, Bohuslav Markalous, put together from various conversations with Loos. Even though this text lacks Loos's usual linguistic virtuosity, since it has been reconstructed from notes taken during the conversations and German was obviously not the editor's mother tongue, we decided to include it in the present volume because it contains important material.

In these late essays Loos refines and develops his attitude to ornamentation and concedes its justification in certain cases, for example to relieve the monotony of manual labor: "A woman who spends eight hours a day standing at the loom . . . feels pleasure, deliverance even when, from time to time, a colored thread appears. It is the colored thread that determines the ornament. Who among us moderns would not call the various, constantly changing fabric patterns modern?" And in the notes to *Ins Leere gesprochen* (Whistling in the Wind) he writes of the book published in 1928 to celebrate the twenty-fifth anniversary of the *Wiener Werkstätte* (a book which he scorned as a "shoddy effort that condemns itself"), "The ornament has been stolen from Sonja Delaunay, an artist I much admire; it was created for printed silk and is very well suited to that (following my theory that things should last as long aesthetically as they last physically)."

In *Österreichs Bau- und Werkkunst* of 1925/26 Loos contributed an appreciation of the wood carver, Franz Zelezny, for his sixtieth birthday. He had already praised his work as exemplary as long ago as 1898, in one of his reports on the Jubilee Exhibition: "Zelezny has not stylized anything. Under his artist-craftsman's hand and eye everything takes on the natural shape of wood. He does not need to start off by mutilating his flowers and leaves on the drawing board; he works directly on the wood, thus giving his ornaments the air of freshness and self-confidence that informs all works of genius. He will not appeal to people who delight in finicky attention to detail. This is not the work of the slaves of antiquity, who were capable of delivering one and the same ornament — astragal or ovolo — by the mile, this is the work of a man of the end of the nineteenth and beginning of the twentieth century, of a man who works out of joy in his own skill, a man who works quickly and productively."

Adolf Loos as a defender of ornamentation? The "enigma that is Loos," of which Nikolaus Pevsner speaks, can be resolved if we look at the interplay between his theories and his practice. He wrote in "Ornament and Education," "By that I did not mean what some purists have carried *ad absurdum*, namely that ornament should be systematically and consistently eliminated. What I did mean was that where it had disappeared as a necessary consequence of human development, it could not be restored, just as people will never return to tattooing their faces." By this time others had long since take over his anti-ornament thesis and radicalized it, so that Loos felt it necessary to distance himself from them, even at the risk of being considered conservative or inconsistent.

"In so doing he stood out against the sloganizing of the partisans of both the newfangled and the oldfangled, with the result that he was not understood." wrote Paul Engelmann, a disciple of Loos who designed the Wittgenstein house, in 1946 in a brochure on Loos. "Anyone who opposes the modernist slogan is a fascist in the eyes of the modernists and anyone who opposes the traditionalist slogan is a Bolshevik in the eyes of the conservatives. But anyone who opposes both at once is a fool in *everyone's* eyes."

His final years were overshadowed not only by illness, but by resignation and bitterness. Loos felt marginalized, misunderstood and ignored. Among his last designs is a sketch for his own tomb. It was to be a smooth, unadorned block of gray granite with the inscription, "ADOLF LOOS, WHO LIBERATED MANKIND FROM SUPERFLUOUS LABOR." No question of ornament here, where he is drawing up a balance of his life's work.

In a call to set up a Loos school — on the occasion of his sixtieth birthday; the signatories were Karl Kraus, Arnold Schoenberg, Heinrich Mann, James Joyce and the French translator of *Ulysses*, Valery Larbaud — he was once more praised as a benefactor of future generations whom he had liberated from superfluous labor: "Though he was the man who triumphed over ornament, his name is passed over and books are written on the history of the fight against ornament without mentioning him. One purpose of this school is to prevent *his logical development of the lack of ornamentation: the cubic method of construction* from falling into the wrong hands and being trivialized."

The Adolf Loos School never materialized. The City of Vienna did carry out Loos's design for his own tomb, but without the inscription Loos wanted. Perhaps it would have led to misunderstandings, given the disastrous unemployment of the 1930s.

There are still some misunderstandings concerning "the enigma that was Loos" to be cleared up, even though as the years go by new books on him and his work appear which help to fill the gaps. The Loos phenomenon is still relevant to us in the twenty-first century. Perhaps one answer as to why interest in Loos continues is contained in Marilaun's brochure on him. After discussing houses, villas, stores and apartments which Loos designed "honestly, according to their function and extremely economi-cally if necessary," Marilaun, with reference to one of these cheaply built Loos houses, declares he has "seen only happy, contented, decent people" in that house. His conclusion: "There is no Loos paradox: his houses build their own people."

Adolf and Daniel Opel

1. A Competition Organized by the City of Vienna (1897)

The City of Vienna invited Viennese architects to submit designs for a pavilion for an exhibition and the results are on display in one of the rooms adjoining the great hall of the Rathaus. The entries are not really worth spending much time on. They are the usual collection of projects, some better, some worse, which any decent draftsman can produce once he knows how to use a pencil and has a long enough back run of *Architektonische Rundschau* and *Deutsche Concurrenzen* available to him. Food for thought, however, is provided by the criteria adopted by the judges in assessing the entries.

Two artists had somehow managed to find their way into this assembly of subscribers to architectural journals. How they got there is a mystery to me. They had no hope of success. Didn't an anonymous pamphlet appear in the course of the year condemning their movement and branding them and their leaders as "materialists"? That was because they were disciples of Semper[1] and put their master's principle that every material speaks its own language into practice. The unscrupulous author of the pamphlet, however, quoted Semper's words out of context and turned them into the opposite. That meant his followers were finished among Viennese architects. Since they had no hope of winning, they perhaps participated merely to say to those Viennese who have not entirely given up hope of seeing art return to the city, "Do not despair. We are still here. When our time comes we will be ready to follow the call."

One of them, Olbrich,[2] was awarded the third prize and the other, Hoffmann[2] a commendation. The first and second prizes went to representatives of the school of assiduous journal-readers.

But one should not imagine that this activity takes up all of these gentlemen's time. Their achievements in another area is also outstanding. I mean in imitation. Walk round the streets and admire all the corbels, dentils and wreaths cast in cement and pinned onto the buildings. Who has not been amazed at the invention of these architects who, to avoid any suspicion of "materialism," paint wooden walls to look like stucco and treat rooms done in stucco like wood! And now a pavilion for an exhibition! What a new field of endeavor opened up to imitation! And no need to worry about those tedious walls, nor about being called a "materialist" by our anonymous author, which was always a danger as long as one left walls as walls. Here there was no likelihood of that! Wood, wood and yet more wood, which — hallelujah! — one could happily treat as blocks of granite. A perfect opportunity for fakery to run riot!

People will object that this was the case with all exhibition buildings so far. Those times are past, I'm afraid, gentlemen, those times are past. The World Exhibition in Chicago was the high point of this trend. It was impossible to take this monumental nonsense any farther and it came to a well-earned end. It had nowhere left to go. Since then exhibition buildings have developed their own style. I need only remind you of the exhibitions in Berlin, Leipzig, Hamburg and Stockholm. This style reached its peak in the current year's exhibition in Tervueren (Belgium), which the leading figures of modern architecture and crafts — van de Velde, Kankar, Serburier-Bovy, and Hobé — used as a dress rehearsal for Paris which is surely unparalleled anywhere. One thing we can say for sure now: this is the style in which all advanced nations will compete in Paris. And our own Jubilee Exhibition will show how we will be represented in Paris, for to set out on a new track *afterwards* is an experiment that has nothing to recommend it. And here the projects of Olbrich and Hoffmann are just what we need. Looking at their work, every art lover must say to himself, if only the authorities would at least try! These projects are Viennese to the very core, Viennese in the effortless harmony of forms. The English details, to which, by the way, I strongly object, only affect superficial aspects. It is honest 'Rabitz architecture'[3] and, as the colored perspective drawing shows, the colored frieze round the base of Olbrich's white plaster walls combined with the green-painted wood of the projecting roof would have produced a perfectly composed ensemble of great charm. If you also take into account the nicely judged height, the way the scale is observed and the generous ground plan, three aspects on which all the entrants, including Hoffmann, have fallen down, then we can see we have an ideal project we would not have believed Vienna capable of producing. Both buildings say, "We are pavilions for an exhibition."

That, however, is what the other projects do not say. Apart from the fact that they pretend to be constructed out of stone and made for eternity, their external appearance tries to deceive us into thinking they are halls of fame, museums, cafés etc. The design that won the first prize, for example, is saying, "I'm a branch of the German *Reichstag*." A flattering newspaper report commented that it was in the style that has become accepted during His Majesty's reign. Correct, but in Prussia! It strikes me as a strange way of paying homage to our monarch to celebrate the fiftieth anniversary of his accession by erecting in the *Prater*[4] a miniaturized pastiche of that prototype of the Greater Prussian architectural style Berliners have aptly nicknamed the *Stampiglienburg*.[5] Don't get me wrong, I'm no dyed-in-the-wool Austrian nationalist, but I'm unhappy when we make fools of ourselves to outsiders in artistic matters. We have no need to deck ourselves out in other people's cast-offs.

The second prize went to a neatly executed representation of a rococo summerhouse. The most self-assured design, however, was the one labeled "To the Burghermaster." It said quite openly, "I am the competition entry that Kuder and Müller, Strasbourg, designed for a hall of fame in Barmen,"[6] and its frankness did not go unrewarded. This was too much for Hoffmann. He saw this commendation as an insult to his own work and in righteous anger tore up the card announcing, in nondescript roundhand, the same dubious award that had been placed over his design.

We can see from this the criteria the jury had adopted. Shallowness, sham, mediocrity were showered with rewards and honors. And our talented artists are . . . are — I'm looking for a polite way or putting it — let's say they are placed on a par with plagiarists. This is our own dirty linen which it would be preferable not to wash in public, but the situation compels me to. Given the forthcoming Paris exhibition, the call should go out to all talented artists to come forward and show what they can do. If our industries lack an elegant, modern shop-window then they will suffer losses to their foreign competitors. We must disprove the old saying that Austria is always one step behind the times. For that is what the jury were, with the honorable exception of Professor Wagner, whom we have to thank for the minor successes (third prize and commendation).

Notes

1. Gottfried Semper (1803-1879), the most important German architect of the mid-nineteenth century; he came to Vienna in 1871.

2. Josef Maria Olbrich (1867-1908), and Josef Hoffmann (1870-1956), two of the leaders of *art nouveau* in Vienna.

3. Rabitz is the inventor [in 1878, M. M.] of the construction method that makes it possible to erect whole buildings from iron, wire mesh and plaster. (footnote in original)

4. A large green space just outside the center of Vienna between the Danube and the Danube Canal which was the site of the Rotunda, built to house the World Exhibition of 1873 and where the exhibition to celebrate Franz Josef's jubilee in 1898 was also held.

5. Literally the "Rubber-stamp castle," presumably either because it was seen as the heart of Prussian bureaucracy or possibly because the four spiky towers at the corners made it look like an upended rubber stamp.

6. See *Deutsche Concurrenzen*, vol. 5, no. 8, p. 33. The design was purchased by the city of Barmen. (footnote in original)

2. From Otto Wagner's Class (1898)

Pletschnik has won the Rome Prize. That is the sensation in the exhibition of students' work — from Professor Otto Wagner's special class on architecture — currently being held in the Academy of Art. Joseph Pletschnik is well known. While still a student at the Academy he repeatedly attracted attention, most recently in winning a prize for the controversial Gutenberg memorial, which unfortunately is not to be carried out, and then again in designing the decoration for the applied arts section of the Lower Austrian Trades Association's exhibit in the Rotunda.[1] People justifiably had high hopes of his class project, but they were disappointed in all respects. Despite that, he was awarded the highest honor, the travel scholarship. It was baffling.

And yet it was right. The prize was awarded not to a square meter of drawing paper, but to the man Pletschnik. And he is a rare man, a man who needs the air of Italy as much as a starving man needs bread. For Pletschnik is the hungriest among our young architects and that is why he must be fed. One thing we can be sure of: whatever he consumes will be returned a thousandfold in energy.

His project is disappointing. That, however, is not to say that it is of poor quality. Perhaps — a thousand thoughts flash through one's mind, one if which is called Richard Wagner — so perhaps . . . It is a bathing establishment for Scheveningen in which the load-bearing frame is completely of iron. There are many designs bearing witness to Pletschnik's imagination in which — and this is another aspect distinguishing him from his fellow students — the main emphasis is no longer placed on perfection of draftsmanship.

After Pletschnik Hubert Gessner is probably the one who had greatest claim on the prize. His work, a grandiose street decoration for a meeting between monarchs — intended for the square between the museums and Ringstraße — is a riot of forms that makes your head reel. Decorative art, that is the forte of the Wagner class — not of Wagner himself, that is by no means the same thing. In a one-off building for a special event one can accept a certain amount of exuberance which one would soon tire of in an apartment block.

Alois Ludwig is exhibiting a decent project for a new academy building, Gustav Roßmann a royal vault. The latter also won the Hansen Prize with a Greek-style garden pavilion.

Among the second-year students Victor Kovacic and Roderich Swoboda stand out. The class project was a hotel on which all the students worked; it is going up at the moment in the block in Magdalenenstraße[2] between the Theater an der Wien and the new *Sezession* building.[3] It would be premature to pass judgment on the first-year students just now.

Former students who are currently abroad on travel scholarships are also exhibiting. Leopold Bauer, who is in Paris at the moment, has contributed a house for an industrial magnate and a concert hall for Beethoven's symphonies. The former is a charming concept, one can clearly see the influence of Bauer's stay in Italy the previous year. On the other hand the Beethoven Hall does not match up to the best of his architecture. He has shown us greater and more complete designs.

The greatest success, however, belongs to Jan Kotera, the winner of last year's Rome Prize. It is only an unassuming pencil drawing and yet it has the embarrassing quality of overwhelming everything around it. It is a temple to Cupid and Psyche. Never has an architect spoken to us in more classical tones, never has an artist expressed himself in more Roman tones. Once more he is the one we find most impressive. Once more one architect, with a grand, simple, classical gesture, has silenced the whole army of ornamentalists with all their violent gesticulation, something that has happened again and again in the history of architecture ever since we have become thoroughly convinced of the superiority of classical culture. The temple to Cupid and Psyche will give rise to a new trend in Viennese architecture. Kotera is a name to remember.

Notes

1. A large building (100 meters in diameter, 85 meters tall at its highest point) with a circular central part surrounded by an arcaded square with four elaborate gateways, situated in the Prater, a park just outside the center of Vienna. It was built by Karl von Hasenauer for the World Exhibition of 1873. The reference here is to an exhibit for the Jubilee Exhibition of 1898.

2. Now the Linke Wienzeile.

3. The *Sezession* was the group representing *art nouveau* in Vienna; the building was designed by Josef Maria Olbrich.

3. A Viennese Architect (1898)

Being most strongly opposed to the movement followed by young artists, and not only in Vienna, I find it difficult to write about JOSEF HOFFMANN. For me tradition is everything, the free exercise of the imagination of secondary importance. In Hoffmann, however, we are dealing with an artist who has, with the help of his fertile imagination, successfully done away with old traditions, and even I have to admit there was much dead wood among them.

It is as an architect that HOFFMANN is most successful. Both his competition design for the City of Vienna pavilion for the Jubilee Exhibition as well as the one for the two apartment blocks in the Mehlmarkt are models of the way the problem of materials should be dealt with here in Vienna. In them the obsession with imitating stone blocks has been completely abandoned and the plaster, on the principle of cladding,[1] covers the exterior without being interrupted by sham joins. HOFF-MANN has thought up an extraordinary effect for the laurel wreaths to be applied to the fresh plaster of the apartment block. The leaves are to be coated with green bronze while the fruits are intended to be low-wattage lamp-bulbs. The way these cement façades go back to the techniques of the old plaster-workers is heartily to be welcomed. On the other hand many people will have mixed feelings to hear that HOFFMANN has declared war on cornices. He believes that with our tall houses they can no longer fulfill their purpose of protecting the whole of the façade from rain.

Although I cannot say I approve of his furniture, one has to bear in mind that things were so bad here that it took a really loud, a really strident blast on the horn to awaken the spirits from their torpor. That is how we should also look on *Ver Sacrum*,[2] for which HOFFMANN has provided many excellent decorations. Now that we have been roused, it is to be hoped that our artists, like *Ver Sacrum*, which with each number is adopting more and more elegant and subdued tones, will treat awakened Vienna more gently.

Notes

1. See the article, "The Principle of Cladding."
2. The periodical of the *Sezession*, the representatives of *art nouveau* in Vienna; it appeared from 1898 to 1903

4. The Potemkin City (1898)

Who has not heard of the villages erected in the Ukraine by Potemkin, that crafty favorite of Catherine the Great? Villages of cardboard and canvas, the purpose of which was to transform a deserted wasteland into a blooming landscape for the eyes of Her Majesty. But a city? Did the crafty minister even create a city?

It could presumably only happen in Russia?

The Potemkin city I am talking about here is our own dear Vienna. A serious accusation, I know, which I will find difficult to prove, since it demands listeners with a keen sense of justice such as are rare in our city.

Someone who claims to be more than he is, is a fraud and is generally despised even if no one suffers loss through it. But what of someone who tries to achieve the same effect through the use of imitation stones and other sham materials? There are countries where he would suffer the same fate. We haven't come that far in Vienna yet. The number of those who feel that this is something immoral, a swindle, is small. And people try to achieve this effect not only with fake watch-chains, not only with their furnishings, which consist of nothing but imitations, but with their homes, the buildings they live in.

Whenever I take a stroll along the Ring I feel as if a modern Potemkin has been trying to make someone believe they have been transported to a city inhabited by no one but the nobility.

Anything and everything that Renaissance Italy produced in the way of aristocratic palaces has been purloined in order to conjure up for His Majesty the Plebs a New Vienna which could only be inhabited by people capable of occupying a whole mansion from foundations to eaves by themselves: the stables on the ground floor, the servants on the low mezzanine, the reception rooms on the high first floor with its wealth of architectural detail and above them the living and sleeping quarters. The Viennese landlord is delighted to own such a property, and the tenant to live in one. Even the ordinary man who has rented a parlor-plus-sleeping-cubicle right at the top feels a *frisson* of lordly grandeur and feudal magnificence when he looks at the house where he lives from outside. Does not the owner of an imitation diamond likewise cast loving glances at the glittering glass? How is the deceiver deceived!

People will object that I am attributing to the Viennese motives they do not possess. It is the architects who are to blame, the architects who should not have built in that manner. I must speak up for architects. Every city gets the architects it deserves. Building styles are regulated by supply and demand. The one who can best meet the wishes of the inhabitants will be the one who designs the most buildings and the most capable architect will perhaps die without ever having attracted a commission. The others set the tone and then people build houses in that style because they happen to have become used to it. And they have to build like that. The property speculator would far prefer to have the façade covered in smooth plaster from top to bottom. That costs the least. And in doing so he would be following an instinct that is right, true and artistic. But people would not want to rent apartments in his house. It is to make it attractive to prospective tenants that the owner is forced to pin this façade, and this one alone, to the building.

Yes, to pin! These Renaissance and Baroque palaces are not even constructed from the materials they appear to be. Some pretend to be built of stone, like Roman and Tuscan palaces, some of plaster, like Viennese Baroque buildings. They are of neither. Their ornamental features, their corbels, wreaths, cartouches and dentils, are cast in cement and pinned on. Of course this technique, which only came into use in the course of this century, has its own validity. But it is not right to use it for forms, the development of which is closely connected with the qualities of a particular material, simply because there are no technical difficulties to stop one using it. The artist's task should be to find a new language for the new material. Anything else is imitation.

That was something the Viennese were not in the least concerned about during the most recent periods of building. In fact they were even pleased to be able to imitate the expensive materials, on which the designs were modeled, at such small expense. As genuine parvenus, they believed other people wouldn't notice. The parvenu always believes that. He is convinced that all the fakes with which he surrounds himself, the false shirt-fronts and imitation furs, fulfill their purpose entirely. But his vain efforts merely elicit a smile from those who have a higher social standing, those who have progressed beyond the parvenu stage. And gradually the parvenu's eyes are opened too. He starts to notice things of his friends' which he had thought were genuine. At that point he gives up in resignation.

Poverty is no disgrace. Not everyone can be born in a baronial hall. But to try and make others think so is ridiculous and immoral. We should stop feeling ashamed of living in the same building as many other people of the same social status. We should stop feeling ashamed of the fact that there are building materials we cannot afford. We should stop feeling ashamed that we are men of the nineteenth century and not ones who live in a house whose style comes from an earlier age. Then you would see how soon our modern age would have its very own architectural style. But we have one already, you will object. But I mean a style we can hand down to posterity with a clear conscience, a style people will still look on with pride, even in the distant future. That is the style Vienna has not found in this century. Whether a Russian prince represents wooden cottages full of happy peasants in canvas, cardboard and paint, or we erect stone palaces, which could be the seat of feudal magnates, out of bricks and cement rendering, the principle is the same. The spirit informing Viennese architecture of the past century is that of Potemkin.

5. To Our Young Architects (1898)

Is architecture still an art? One is tempted to answer in the negative. Neither within the artistic community nor among the public at large is the architect regarded as a real artist. The most insignificant of painters, the most minor of sculptors, the poorest of actors and the most unperformed of composers all claim the title of artist, and the world accords it them unquestioningly. But an architect must have outstanding achievements to show before he is accepted into the ranks of the artists.

Two factors have worked to undermine architects' prestige. The first is the state, the second architects themselves. The state has introduced examinations at the technical universities and those who have passed these examinations believe that gives them the right to use the term "architect" as a title. This farce has gone so far that there were those who wanted to petition the government to bring in regulations restricting the use of the designation "architect" to graduates of the structural engineering departments of the technical universities. That the whole of educated Vienna did not burst out into loud and liberating laughter is sufficient proof, if proof be needed, of the extent to which these examinations have given rise to the general opinion that architecture is something that can be learned, its mastery proved by a diploma. To see how ridiculous this is, we just need to transfer the whole affair to music. Imagine that the graduates of the conservatory demanded that only those who had passed an examination there be allowed to practice composition, which is, after all, closely related to the architect's creative work. Music is still regarded as an absolute art.

For the true artist, the arguments used by the title-obsessed graduates of the technical universities were totally spurious. "At the moment any bricklayer's apprentice can call himself an architect." Why not, if he wants to? Does it dim the glory of Beethoven and Wagner that a man who writes a music-hall song also calls himself a composer? Have Lenbach[1] and Menzel[2] ever been harmed by the fact that the craftsman who paints a house is called a painter? Of course not. But wouldn't they have looked ridiculous if they had demanded state protection for the designation "painter"? I can hardly bring myself to suggest it, even as a hypothetical example.

But even more than the examinations, it is architects who have harmed themselves. They have downgraded themselves and the world has reacted accordingly. Despite the title they insist on and their artistic ability, most of our young architects are nothing more than architectural draftsmen. For a salary equal to that of a poorly paid, not particularly competent clerk, they work for builders and architects who can afford to set up their own studio. Their working hours are those of a commercial employee as well. Whether their artistic outlook coincides with that of their employer is a matter of complete indifference to these "architects." Most of them have none at all, anyway. One day they are working in the Gothic style, while in their next situation they have to show enthusiasm for the Italian Renaissance. And they agree with everything. True, among their like-minded cronies they make fun of their boss — note the commercial vocabulary architects are already using — and think no end of themselves as they pull the old fogey to pieces. And the next morning they are back at work on the dot of eight.

If the younger generation of artists had the moral courage to stand up for their convictions despite the financial disadvantages, then the standing of our art would be very quick to improve. Look at your colleagues in painting, sculpture and music. They are willing, if necessary, to starve for their art. That is what qualifies a man for the finest title our nation has to give: artist.

Notes

1. Franz von Lenbach (1836-1904), active in Munich, the most successful German portrait-painter of his day.

2. Adolf von Menzel (1815-1905), active in Berlin; important both as a painter and an illustrator.

6. The Old and the New Style in Architecture: A Parallel with Special Reference to the Artistic Situation in Vienna (1898)

It seems to me that, as far as adaptation to current trends is concerned, architecture comes last among the visual arts. That is easy to explain. A picture, an engraving, a sculpture has its origin in a flash of inspiration and the work can be sent out into the world in a matter of weeks or months. It is different with architecture. The preparatory work alone demands years of intellectual and artistic activity and a whole lifetime can be spent on carrying it out.

The changes that have already taken place in the other arts make it all the easier for us to predict the future paths architecture will take. Being an art concerned with form and space (I reject the view that would place it among the graphic arts), architecture will be particularly influenced by sculpture. There is a development in society which has made itself felt in the course of the century and which is already affecting sculpture: manual work has come back into favor.

Even very recently we lived in a strange age in which brain-work was everything, handwork nothing. However good he was at his work, as far as social status was concerned the man in the blue apron stood far below the poorly-paid pen-pusher. The arts were also affected by this madness: wherever possible any actual physical task was left to the craftsman, who was expected to follow the artist's designs slavishly. That wasn't possible in painting, of course, but the sculptor only worked on maquettes. The actual work of *sculpting*, the technical mastery over the material, remained foreign to him. And architects remained tied to their offices, sometimes drawing up their designs without even having seen the site for their artistic endeavors. They left everything to the craftsmen. True, the more assiduous among them would go to the construction site and swear and curse at the stupidity of the craftsmen, who of course had not managed to carry out all the intentions contained in their designs to the letter — but only

after it was too late for any changes. They simply ignored the fact that the manual worker is a human being, not a machine.

It was above all the English who did away with the idea that handwork is something inferior. If you want to make a pot, don't draw a solid of revolution, sit down at the wheel. If you want to make a chair, don't spend ages at the drawing-board, pick up a plane. They took the artist into the workshop and told him to get on with it.

And then came the reaction. Whereas it had previously been considered rather vulgar to work in a workshop, now it was all the rage. "The sculptor, Mr A. N. Other, at work carving out his bust of Danae in variegated marble." It has a ring to it, doesn't it? Pure Renaissance. The artist who was not afraid to pick up hammer and chisel and learn the stonemason's trade became the focus of attention. He was more rather than, as previously, less highly regarded than his colleagues who only made drawings and models. The number of sculptors who were unwilling to leave the execution of their works to a mindless copying machine or a practicing sculptor who might have ideas of his own grew and grew.

Architecture, too, will have to come to terms with this demand of the modern age. The architect will do more of his work at the building site. He will only consider the decoration when the space is completed and the lighting can be determined. The time-consuming and completely superfluous task of drawing ornamental details will no longer be necessary. The architect-craftsman will have models of the decoration made in the workshop from sketches, perhaps even at the construction site itself, and put the finishing corrections in with his own hand after having made a close study of the lighting and the distance from the observer. That will, of course, take up more of his time, with the result that he will build less. The large architectural offices ("house-factories" to be more precise) will disappear.

But what will buildings constructed in this way look like? I think we can assume they will look much more conservative than they appear in the dreams of our young radicals. Architecture is based on feelings and habits which are constantly being influenced by existing buildings, which belong to all the millennia.

What is it the architect actually does? He uses materials to arouse feelings in us which are not inherent in those materials themselves. He builds a church. People should be put in a reverent mood. He builds a bar. People should feel at ease there. How do you do that? You see what buildings aroused those feelings in the past. That is where you must start out from because for their whole lives people have prayed in certain rooms, drunk in others. The feeling is acquired, not innate, and an architect, if he is at all serious about his art, must take these acquired feelings into account.

One would imagine that things that gave us pleasure five hundred years ago would have lost the power to do so today. That is true. A tragedy that moved us to tears then would be no more than interesting today. A joke from those days would hardly even raise a smile now. The tragedy is not performed any more, the joke is forgotten. But the building remains, surrounded by a changing posterity, and that explains why, despite all the changes in outlook, architecture will always be the conservative art.

For there is one feeling we simply cannot expunge from our memory: the superiority of classical antiquity. Since that was revealed to us, all Gothic, Moorish, Chinese styles etc have lost their power over us. They may well influence a stylistic renewal, and have ever done so, but there will always come a great mind, I like to call him the super-architect, who will free architecture of foreign elements and return us to pure, classical forms. And the public always greets this man with rejoicing, for our hearts and minds are imbued with classicism. After the great architects of the Italian Renaissance there were in Germany countless minor masters full of good ideas, overflowing with imagination. Who now remembers their names? Then came Schlüter in the north, Fischer von Erlach in the south, Le Pautre in France,[1] men of a classical Roman sensibility who brought us another high point. And after that things once more went downhill, once more all classes succumbed to an unbridled delight in a wealth of different forms, producing architects whose names are now known only to academic research. Then Schinkel[2] appeared, the man who tamed untrammeled imagination, followed, after another downhill slide, by Semper. From this we can see that the architect who is revered by posterity is the one who makes fewest concessions to his own age, who is the most uncompromising advocate of the classical point of view. For architects do not create works for their times alone, later periods are entitled to find pleasure in them as well. This requires a fixed, unchanging standard which for the present and the future, unless some great cataclysm brings about a complete change in values, is classical antiquity.

Two things, then, are now clear: the architect of the future will be involved in the actual construction process and he will be trained in classicism. One can even say that of all professions architecture is the one that demands the strictest classical training. In order, however, to be able to satisfy the material needs of his times, he must also be a modern man. He must not merely have a thorough understanding of the cultural needs of his contemporaries, he must stand at the forefront of that culture. For he has it in his power, through his conception of a ground plan, through the design of fittings and furnishings, to put a different stamp on certain forms and usages of his culture. It is, therefore, incumbent on him to make sure any changes are for the better, never for the worse.

The architect of the future must also be a gentleman. The times are past when it is sufficient not to steal to be regarded as honorable. Aristides, had he lived today, would not have been admired for his poverty. This is something we take for granted. We are becoming more and more sensitive to questions of right and wrong, with the logical consequence that architects are expected not to try to deceive people with regard to materials. Of course, this expectation will automatically be fulfilled when the architect himself has to translate his design into material. For the craftsman does not practice this deception. It was the draftsman-architect who introduced it into architecture.[3] Since, however, an architect cannot master all materials (in fact each person can only master one), they will start to specialize, as was the custom in earlier times: architect in stone (stonemason[4]), architect in brick (bricklayer), architect in stucco (plasterer) and architect in wood (carpenter). You want a stone church? Right, you go to the stonemason. You want a brick barracks? The bricklayer builds it. You want a house with plaster rendering? You commission it from a plasterer. You want a wood ceiling in your diningroom? The carpenter makes it.

Yes, but — you will object — what about the artistic unity of the whole design? I deny that any such thing is necessary. No one can deny that in the old days magnificent buildings were created using the method I describe. A building in which all the details, right down to the keyplates, are the product of *one* mind, will lose all its freshness; it will be boring. Always the same ornament, always the same molding, a bit bigger here, a bit smaller there, on the façade, over the entrance, in the hall, in the mosaic floor, on the lamps, on the wall-covering. Take the Golden Hall in Augsburg town hall. Is it not a magnificent room? And it was created by two artists: a master builder, Elias Holl, who was responsible for the interior, and a master carpenter, Wolfgang Ebner, who created the wonderful ceiling. But with this division of labor, the "artistic unity of the whole" is an illusion. How often do two or even three architects join to create a firm and leave the actual execution to an army of draftsmen? How easy would it not be to modify this so that an artist, the boss, sketches out the design and leaves the details to draftsmen who have learned a craft. The boss will, of course, have corrections to put in, but he will also be willing to bow to the expert judgment of his colleague. The artist himself will, however, have had to master one of the four crafts mentioned above.

In this essay I have concentrated on what can be achieved, given our present outlook, without getting involved in utopian lines of thought. These ideas are meant for the present and the immediate future. Whether a social revolution will bring about new forms and ideas is something I did not think it necessary to go into. The world today is still ruled by capitalism and it is for that system alone that my remarks are intended.

Notes

1. Andreas Schlüter, ca. 1660-1714; Johann Bernhard Fischer von Erlach,1656-1723; Antoine Le Pautre,1621-1682.

2. Karl Friedrich Schinkel, 1781-1841, mainly active in Prussia, the greatest German architect of the nineteenth century.

3. One occasionally comes across objections to this which appear to have some justification. What about the *stuccolustro* work of the Italian Renaissance, someone might ask, that is surely a straightforward imitation of marble? My response to that would be that the old craftsmen were not so much trying to imitate the actual material as the magnificent patterning of the marble. The stonemason does the same when he tries to translate an acanthus-leaf or a garland into his material. And, unlike their modern counterparts, the old craftsmen *never* tried to imitate hairline joins. On the contrary, they saw the opportunity of working on large surfaces without joins as an *advantage* over genuine marble. For me that is genuine pride in one's craft, in contrast to our modern plasterers, who to me seem like poor forgers who are constantly afraid of being caught in the act. (footnote in original)

4. What greatness lies in the title, "Friedrich Schmidt, a German stonemason." It is well known that Schmidt, who worked as master builder on a cathedral [St. Stephen's in Vienna — M. M.], rejected the designation "architect." He always emphasized the fact that he was a craftsman. (footnote in original)

7. Building Materials (1898)

What is worth more, a kilogram of stone or a kilogram of gold? Ridiculous question. But only for a merchant. A great artist will say, "To me all materials are equally valuable."

The Venus de Milo would be equally valuable whether it were made of road-metal — in Paros Parian marble is used for road foundations — or gold. The Sistine Madonna would not be worth a penny more if Raphael had mixed a few pounds of gold in with his paints. A merchant, who has to bear in mind the possibility of melting down the golden Venus or scraping off the Sistine Madonna, will presumably be of a different opinion.

But the artist is fired by one ambition alone: to master the material in such a way that his work is independent of the value of the raw material. Our architects, however, do not have this ambition. For them a square meter of wall in granite is more valuable than the same area in mortar.

And yet granite is intrinsically worthless. It is lying around in the fields and anyone can take it. Or there are whole mountains of it, whole mountain ranges, just waiting to be quarried out. We use it for road-metal, we use it for cobblestones. It is the commonest stone, the most ordinary material we know. And yet there are people who consider it a valuable building material?

When these people say material, they mean labor. Human labor, skill and art. Granite requires a great deal of labor to remove it from the mountain, a great deal of labor to bring it to where it is needed, labor to shape it, labor to grind and polish it and make it look attractive. Looking at a wall of polished granite, we are filled with awe. Not at the material, at the labor that has gone into it.

Does that mean granite is more valuable than mortar after all? Not necessarily. A stucco wall with decorations by Michelangelo will outshine the best polished granite. It is not only the quantity but also the quality of labor involved that goes toward determining the value of an object.

We are living in a time which lays greater emphasis on the

quantity of labor. It is easier to monitor and is immediately obvious to everyone, not requiring a practiced eye or specialized knowledge; there is no possibility of error. So many day-laborers worked on it for so many hours at so much per hour. Everyone can work it out. And we want to make it easy for everyone to see the value of the things we surround ourselves with, otherwise there would be no point in having them. That explains why those materials are more highly regarded which demand more hours of labor to produce them.

That has not always been the case. In former times people used those materials which were most easily obtainable. In some areas that was brick, in others stone, in yet others the walls were covered with mortar. And did those who built in this fashion feel themselves inferior to the architect who worked in stone? Why ever should they? Such an idea never occurred to anybody. Had there been a quarry nearby, they would have built in stone, but to bring stone from far away seemed to them more a question of money than of art. And in the old days art, that is, the quality of the work, was more highly valued than today.

Such periods also produced strong-minded characters in the field of architecture. Fischer von Erlach did not need granite to make himself understood. He created works out of clay, lime-stone and sand which move us as powerfully as buildings made from more recalcitrant substances. The most lowly material responded to his artistic genius. A king in the realm of materials, he had the ability to raise plebeian dust to the nobility of art.

However, architecture today is dominated not by the artist but by the day-laborer, not by creative ideas but by hours of work. And even the dominance of the day laborer is gradually being eroded through the appearance of a better and cheaper supplier of the quantitative labor output: the machine.

But every hour of work, whether it is provided by the laborer or the machine, costs money. And if you have no money? You start faking the amount of labor involved, you start imitating materials.

This reverence for quantity in labor is the worst enemy of

craftsmen, since it leads to imitation and imitation has demoralized a large part of our craftsmen. They have lost all pride in their craft. "Printer, what can you do?" — "I can print so you'd think it was a lithograph." — "Joiner, what can you do?" — "I can cut out ornaments so they look as flowing as if they had been made by a plasterer." — "Plasterer, what can you do?" — "I can imitate cornices and ornaments so precisely, with hairline joins anyone would think genuine, that they look like the best stonemason's work." — "I can do that too," the plumber says with pride. "If you paint my ornaments and spray them with sand no one would imagine they were made of lead." What a pathetic bunch!

Our craftsmen have been infected with a spirit of self-denigration, so it is hardly surprising they are not doing very well. But these people are not there to "do well." Come on, joiner, be proud to be a joiner. Yes, the plasterer also makes ornaments. Don't envy him and wish you could do the same, ignore him! And you, plasterer, what is the stonemason to you? The stonemason makes joins, has to make joins, unfortunately, because small blocks are cheaper than large ones. Be proud that your work is free of these paltry joins, that score the columns, ornaments and walls, be proud of your profession, be glad you're not a stonemason.

But I am whistling in the wind. The public does not want proud craftsmen. The better they can imitate, the more support they receive from the public. This is the inevitable consequence of the awe in which expensive materials are held, a sure indication of the parvenu stage our society has reached. Once he knows that diamonds, furs and stone façades cost a lot of money, a parvenu feels ashamed not to be able to deck himself out in diamonds, ashamed not to be able to wear furs, ashamed not to live in a stone palace. What he does not know is that elegance is unaffected by the absence of diamonds, furs or stones. Since he lacks money, he resorts to substitutes. A ridiculous undertaking. The people he wants to deceive, those who do have the means to surround themselves with diamonds, furs and stone façades, cannot be fooled. They are merely amused by his efforts, which are unnecessary to impress those of a lower social standing, as long as one is confident in one's own superiority.

During the last decades the whole of the building industry has been dominated by imitation. Wallpaper is, of course, made from paper, but God forbid that it should show it. It had to be given the look of damask, tapestry or a carpet pattern. Doors and windows are made of softwood, but since hardwood is more expensive, they had to be painted to look like that. Iron was painted with bronze or copper to imitate those metals. But Portland cement, an invention of this century, they had no idea what to do with. A magnificent material in its own right, they had only one idea when thinking about how to use it, the first idea that occurs to them with every new material: what can one imitate with it? It was used as a substitute for stone. And since cement is so exceptionally cheap, people in true parvenu style made lavish use of it. The world was in the grip of a cement craze. "Oh please," pretentious clients would beg their architect, "can't you add another five crowns worth to the façade?" And the architect would pin as many crowns' worth of art to the façade as he was asked to, and sometimes a little bit more.

At the moment cement castings are used to imitate stucco work. It is typical of Vienna that a man who has protested vigorously against this abuse of materials, against imitation, has been branded a materialist. Just consider the contradiction: these are the very same people who place such a high value on materials they will stoop to any dubious practice, even using substitutes to imitate them.

The English have sent us their wallpapers. Unfortunately they cannot send us whole houses, but from the wallpapers alone we can see the English approach. These are wallpapers that are not ashamed they are made of paper. And why should they be? Certainly there are wall-coverings that cost more. But an Englishman is not a parvenu. His house never makes you think he hadn't enough money for what he really wanted. And the cloth he wears is made of sheep's wool and says so openly. If the

Viennese were to take the lead in clothing, wool would be woven to look like velvet or satin. English cloth, that is, the cloth we use, never has the Viennese "I'd-love-to-but-I-can't" look, even though it is made of "mere" wool.

This brings us to the topic that plays the most important role in architecture, the principle that should be the ABC of every architect, the principle of cladding, which I will deal with in my next article.

8. The Principle of Cladding (1898)

If, for an artist, all materials are equally valuable, that does not mean they are equally suitable for all purposes. Stability and practicality demand materials which may not harmonize with the function of the building. Say the architect is to create a warm, cozy room. Carpets are warm and cozy, so he decides to spread one over the floor and hang up four to make the four walls. But you cannot build a house from carpets. Both floor carpets and wall hangings need a construction to keep them in place. Designing this construction is the architect's second task.

That is the correct way, the logical way architects should go about their business. That was the order in which mankind learned to build. In the beginning we sought to clad ourselves, to protect ourselves from the elements, to keep ourselves safe and warm while sleeping. We sought to cover ourselves. Originally con-sisting of animal furs or textiles, this covering is the earliest architectural feature.[1] It had to be fixed somewhere if it was to provide sufficient protection for the whole family. Soon walls were added, to provide protection at the side. And that is the order in which the idea of building developed, both in the individual and in mankind as a whole.

There are architects who do it the other way round. Their imagination creates not rooms but walls, the rooms being the spaces left inside the walls. Then they clad the internal walls with the material that seems most appropriate. That is the empirical route to art.

The true artist, the great architect, however, first of all gets a feeling for the effect he wants to produce and then sees in his mind's eye the rooms he wants to create. The effect he wants to arouse in the observer — for example fear and terror in a dungeon, divine awe in a church, respect for the power of the state in a government building, reverence in a funeral monument, homeliness in a house, cheerfulness in a tavern — comes from the materials used and the form.

Each and every material has its own vocabulary of forms and no material can appropriate the forms of another. Forms develop out of the way a particular material is produced and the ways in which it can be worked, they develop with and out of the material. No material willingly suffers an intruder among its forms and anyone who thrusts one on it will be branded as a forger. But art has nothing to do with forgery, with falsehood. The path of art is thorny but pure.

One could cast the tower of St. Stephen's in cement and set it up somewhere, but that wouldn't make it a work of art. And what is true of the tower of St. Stephen's is true of the Pitti Palace, and what is true of the Pitti Palace is true of the Farnese Palace. And with that building we are right in the middle of our Ringstraße[2] architecture. Sad times for art, sad times for the few artists among the architects who were forced to prostitute their art for the common herd. Only very few were lucky enough to find clients with the generosity of spirit to give the artist his head. The most fortunate was Schmidt,[3] after him Hansen,[4] who, when things were going badly for him, sought comfort in terracotta. What torments Ferstel[5] must have gone through when, at the last minute, he was compelled to pin on whole sections of the façade of his University building in cast cement. The other architects of the period, with few exceptions, were free of such hyper-sensitivity.

Have things changed? I would rather not answer that question. Architecture is still dominated by imitation and substitute materials. And there is worse. In recent years there have even been people prepared to defend it (one, it is true, anonymously; he was obviously not entirely happy with the matter) so that the imitation architect no longer feels it necessary to keep a low profile. Now they calmly pin their "construction" onto the façade and feel they have aesthetic justification in hanging their key"stone" below the main cornice. Come along, come along, all you champions of imitation, you creators of stenciled inlays, house-ugliful windows and papier-mâché tankards, a new field awaits your talents in Vienna, the ground has been freshly manured.

But is a living room that is lined all round with carpets not an imitation? The walls are not built of carpet! Of course they aren't. But these carpets do not claim to be anything other then carpets. They do not pretend, either in color or in pattern, to be masonry but make their function as cladding for the wall surface clear. They fulfill their purpose according to the principle of cladding.

As I said at the start, cladding is older than construction. There are manifold reasons for cladding. It can be for protection against the elements, as with oil-based paint on exterior wood, iron or stone; it can be for hygienic reasons, as with the glazed tiles covering the walls in the toilet; it can be the means of producing some specific effect, as with the colored paint on statues, paper on the walls, a veneer on wood. The principle of cladding, first formulated by Semper, also extends to nature. Human beings are clad with skin, trees with bark.

There is a very precise law behind the principle of cladding. No cause for alarm. Laws, it is generally said, kill off any development. And didn't the old masters get on very well without laws? Certainly. But where theft is unknown there is no point in promulgating laws against it. When the materials used for cladding were not imitations no one wasted their time thinking up laws. Now, however, it seems to me to be high time.

This law runs as follows: there should be no possibility of confusing the cladding with the material it covers. To give a specific example, wood can be painted any color apart from wood color. In a city whose Exhibition Committee decided to paint the old wood in the Rotunda "to look like mahogany" and where graining is the only painting technique used on wood, that is a very bold statement. There seem to be people here who think it is refined. I do not agree. Nor do I find it beautiful. Since the railroad and streetcar carriages come, like all coach-building, from England, these are the only wooden objects here painted in true colors. And I make so bold as to declare that I like these streetcars — especially those of the electric line — with their true colors better than I would if, following the Exhibition Committee's aesthetic principle, they were painted to look like mahogany.

But the people here do possess a true sense of refinement, even if it is mostly lying dormant. Otherwise the railway company would not appeal to it by painting their third-class coaches brown, that is in wood color, rather than the more refined green of their first-class and second-class coaches.

I once demonstrated this unconscious sense to one of my colleagues in a graphic manner. There was a house with two apartments on the first floor. The tenant of the one had had the window frames, which were grained, painted white at his own expense. We made a bet and took a certain number of people to see the house and asked them, without pointing out the difference in the window frames, which apartment they thought belonged to Herr Blunzengruber and which to Prince Liechtenstein (both, it should be added, imaginary tenants). They were unanimous in declaring the wood-grained side Herr Blunzengruber's. Since then my colleague has all his wood painted white.

Wood-graining is, of course, an invention of this century. In the Middle Ages wood was generally painted bright yellow, in the Renaissance blue, in the Rococo interior wood white, exterior green. Our peasants have retained enough common sense still to use true colors. Don't the green doors, green fences and green shutters look charming against the background of a freshly whitewashed wall out in the country? Unfortunately there are some places there which have already adopted the taste of our Exhibition Committee.

You will remember the moral outrage among the craftsmen of the imitation camp when the first pieces of painted furniture arrived from England. It was not against painting as such that these honest fellows directed their fury. As soon as softwoods came into use, people in Vienna also protected them with oil-based paints. What really got these poor fellows up in arms was the brazen way the English furniture openly showed its paint, instead of trying to imitate hardwood. They turned their eyes to heaven and behaved as if they had never used paint. Presumably these gentlemen think that up to now people have taken their wood-grained furniture and fittings for hardwood and I am sure they will be grateful to me that in revealing the practice of painting I do not name names.

Applied to plasterwork, the principle of cladding would run as follows: plaster can be shaped into any ornament except one — brickwork. One would have thought that was a matter of course and didn't need saying, but only recently someone showed me a building with plastered walls which had been colored red and given white joins. The popular kitchen decoration imitating stone blocks comes under this heading too. No materials which are used to clad walls — wallpaper, oilcloth, fabrics and tapestry, that is — should have patterns of bricks or stone.

A material used for cladding may retain its own natural color even if the material it is covering has the same color. I can paint black iron with pitch, I can cover wood with another wood (veneer, inlay etc.) without having to color the covering layer of wood; I can coat one metal with another either by firing or by galvanizing. But the principle of cladding states that no pigment should be added to imitate the material underneath. Therefore iron can be tarred, painted or galvanized, but never bronzed, that is, covered with a metallic paint.

Blocks made of fireclay or artificial stone are also relevant to this argument, being used to imitate in the one case terrazzo (mosaic) floors, in the other Persian carpets. I'm sure there are people who are taken in — the factories will know their clientele.

But no, you are wrong, all you imitation-and-substitute architects. The soul is too high, too sublime to be taken in by your devices and petty ploys. True, you have our bodies in your power. They have only five senses to rely on to distinguish genuine from false. And where human senses fail, that is where your domain begins. Paint your best inlays high, high up on the ceiling and our poor eyes will accept them for what they appear to be. But the divine soul does not believe your fraud. Even in the best of your "looks-just-like-an-inlay" stencils all it will feel is paint.

Notes

1. In this paragraph Loos is exploiting the various meanings of the German word *Decke*: cover, blanket, ceiling.

2. The wide boulevard round the center of Vienna built on the site of the fortifications, which were removed in 1858-60. The grandiose buildings lining it are in a hodgepodge of historical styles.

3. Schmidt was the architect of the *Rathaus*, the city hall.

4. Theophil von Hansen, 1813-1891, a Danish architect who settled in Vienna in 1846. Of the Ringstraße buildings he was responsible for the Academy of Arts (Italian Cinquecento), the Parliament (Greek classical) and the Stock Exchange (Renaissance).

5. Before the University building in Renaissance style Heinrich von Ferstel, 1828-1883, had designed the nearby Gothic Votivkirche.

9. The Story of the Poor Little Rich Man (1900)

I want to tell you the story of a poor little rich man. He had wealth and possessions, a faithful wife, whose kisses smoothed the cares of business from his brow, and a flock of children the poorest of his workers would have envied him. He was loved by his friends, respected by society. Everyone envied him since everything he undertook prospered. Today, however, things are quite, quite different. This is how it happened.

One day the man said to himself, "You have wealth and possessions, a faithful wife and children your poorest worker would envy you. But are you happy, really happy? There are people who lack all the things they envy you, but they have a great sorceress to drive away their cares: Art. What is Art to you? Any swaggering poseur can leave his card and your servant will throw open the door to him, but you have never yet had Art in your home. I know very well she won't come of her own accord. I will go to her. I'll build her a home fit for a queen and get her to come and live with me."

He was a man of vigor. Everything he tackled he carried through with great energy. You could see that in all his business dealings. So that very same day he went to a famous architect and said, "Bring Art to me, I want Art within my own four walls. The cost is irrelevant."

The architect didn't need to be told twice. He went to the rich man's house and threw out all his furniture, brought in an army of parquet-layers, French polishers, masons, decorators, cabinetmakers, plumbers, locksmiths, potters, carpet-fitters, painters and sculptors and in no time at all Art was housed safe and sound in the rich man's home.

The rich man was overjoyed as he went round his new rooms. Wherever he looked there was Art, Art in anything and everything. He held Art in his hand when he took hold of the doorknob, he was sitting on Art when he sat down on a chair, his head reposed on Art when he wearily lay it on the pillow, his foot sank into Art when he walked across the carpets. With the intensity of passion, he reveled in Art. Since his plates boasted an

Artistic decoration he took twice the pleasure in cutting up his *boeuf à l'oignon*.

People praised him, people envied him. The art magazines hailed him as a leading patron, pictures of his rooms were analyzed and interpreted as models to be followed.

And they deserved to be. Each room was a symphony of color complete in itself. Walls, furniture and fabrics harmonized in the most subtle manner. Each article had its place and formed the most marvelous combinations with the others. The architect had not forgotten the least thing. Ashtrays, cutlery, candle-snuffers — he had composed everything, but everything. And it wasn't just common-or-garden architectural decoration. Every ornament, every form, every nail expressed the individuality of its owner. A psychological task the difficulty of which everyone will appreciate.

But the architect modestly waved aside all accolades. For, he said, these rooms are not by me. Over there in the corner is a statuette by Charpentier. And just as I would object to someone claiming a room as his own design if he used just one of my door-handles, so I cannot claim this room as my intellectual property. How consistent, how nobly said! Many a cabinetmaker who had papered the walls of a room with a Walter Crane paper, yet insisted on claiming the furniture as his own just because he had designed and made it, must have felt thoroughly ashamed of himself when he heard those words.

But let us return to our rich man. I have already said how happy he was. From now on he spent a large part of his time studying his home. And he soon realized living in it needed practice. Every object had its own particular place. The architect had done more than could be expected, he had thought of everything in advance. The tiniest box had its special place which was made just for it.

Comfortable his apartment certainly was, but it did tax the brain. For that reason, during the first few weeks the architect supervised the rich man, so that no errors should creep in. The rich man did his best, but it still happened that when he was finished with a book he would be so preoccupied he put it into the compartment designed for newspapers. Or he would tap off the ash from his cigar into the depression in the table intended for the candelabra. Once you had picked up an object it took no end of puzzling and searching to find the place it had come from, sometimes even the architect had to unroll the detail drawings to find where the matchbox belonged.

With applied art making such a splash, something had to be done for applied music. The rich man devoted a lot of time to this matter and submitted a request to the streetcar corporation asking them to instruct their conductors to replace their tuneless ringing with the bell motif from *Parsifal*. Unfortunately the corporation proved uncooperative, they were not yet ready for modern ideas. On the other hand he was allowed to have the cobblestones outside his house relaid, at his own expense, so that every vehicle drove past in the rhythm of the *Radetzky March*, and the electric bells in his house played motifs from Beethoven and Wagner. All the critics were full of praise for the man who had opened up a new field for "art in everyday life."

As one can well imagine, all these improvements made the man even happier.

It has to be admitted, however, that he preferred to be at home as little as possible. One needs a rest from all that art now and then, doesn't one? Or would you like to live in a picture gallery? Or sit through *Tristan and Isolde* for months on end? There you are! Who can blame him if he went to the café, the restaurant, or to visit friends and acquaintances to gather his strength for his home. Art demands sacrifices. And he had made so many. A tear crept into his eye as he thought of all the old things he had been so fond of that he sometimes missed. The big armchair! His father had always taken his afternoon nap in it. And the old clock! The old pictures! But it was all for the sake of Art. Stick to it!

Once he had his birthday. His wife and children had showered him with presents, things that gave him heartfelt pleasure, things that he really liked. Not long after, the architect arrived to make sure everything was all right and to give his ruling in certain tricky questions. He came into the room. The rich man was pleased to see him, for there were many things he wanted to ask. But the architect did not see the look of pleasure on his face, he had noticed something else. "What are those slippers you're wearing?" he gasped.

The rich man looked down at his embroidered slippers. And gave a sigh of relief. This time he was sure of his innocence. They had been made to the architect's own design. "Have you forgotten already?" he asked teasingly. "You designed them yourself!"

"I certainly did," thundered the architect. "For the bedroom! Those two impossible splotches of color ruin the whole ensemble. Can't you see that?"

The rich man could see that. He quickly took his slippers off and was mightily relieved the architect didn't object to his socks as well. They went to the bedroom where the rich man was allowed to put his slippers back on.

"It was my birthday yesterday," he began hesitantly, "and my family have literally showered me with presents. I asked you to come so you could advise us where best to put all the things."

The architect's face grew visibly longer as he listened. Then the storm broke. "What do you think you are doing, getting presents given you? Have I not designed everything for you? Have I not thought of everything? You don't need anything else. You are complete."

"But," the rich man ventured to reply, "surely I can buy myself something?"

"No you may not. Never! That's all I needed, things I didn't design! Isn't it enough that I allowed you the Charpentier statuette that robbed me of all the glory of my work? No, you may not buy anything else."

"But what if my grandson gives me something he made at kindergarten?"

"You don't accept it."

The rich man was shattered. But still he didn't give up. He

had an idea, yes, an idea. "And if I were to buy a picture at the *Sezession?*" He thought he had caught the architect out.

"Then try and find somewhere to put it. Can't you see there's no room left for anything? Can't you see that for every picture I hung up for you I composed a frame on the wall, let into the wall. You can't even move one of the pictures. Just try to find somewhere to put another picture!"

At that a change came over the rich man. He no longer felt happy, he felt deeply unhappy. He could see his future life before him. No one could give him a little surprise any more. He would have to suppress all desire to buy as he walked past the shops; nothing was being produced for him any more. None of his nearest and dearest could give him a picture; painters, artists, craftsmen did not exist for him any longer. He was shut out of all future life and longing, all striving and struggle. The time had come, he felt, to learn how to go round with his own corpse. Yes, he's finished. He is complete.

10. Guided Tours of Apartments (1907)

For two years now people have been saying modern house furnishing has run out of ideas. People have been saying we should go back to older styles. The *Biedermeier*[1] is prescribed as the ultimate remedy.

In Germany the modern movement was called *Jugendstil*, here in Austria *Sezession*. Both words have become terms of abuse.

It is ten years ago now that I wrote a series of articles warning against these two styles. I said at the time that our furnishings should be in neither one of the old nor one of the new styles, but modern.

Then I was in a minority, a very small minority indeed. A minority of one.

Our modern products were treated with contempt, both by artists and by the authorities. I pointed out that it was not necessary to develop a style for our times since it already existed. Our machines, our clothes, our carriages and harnesses, our glassware and metalware, in fact everything that had managed to escape "improvement" by our architects, was modern. It is true that joiners and cabinetmakers have been under the architect's thumb for the last fifty years. The important thing, then, was to free them from the architect's frills and furbelows. Then we would not have far to go to get modern room furnishings.

To do that was very simple. Certain of the joiner's products had escaped the "improving" hand of the architect and it was these that had to be gathered and their forms applied to similar structures. There were the compartmented trays used to carry round cigars in Viennese restaurants; there were the iceboxes for ice cream in Viennese cafés; there were the glass showcases in stores; there were the mountings used on them, the metal fittings on suitcases. Even the wooden housing for water closets showed how wall paneling might be developed.

Now we had modern joinery. What it lacked was what required the collaboration of an architect: ornament. Old furniture had had carved or inlaid ornamentation, and since the modern cabinetmaker cannot design it he had to rely on the architect. The cabinetmaker cannot design ornaments because he is a modern man. The architect could and can because he is not modern. For — and this is something else I said ten years ago — a modern man is no longer capable of producing ornament. The modern products of our culture have no ornamentation. Suitcase makers, leatherworkers, tailors, electricians and machine manufacturers do not ornament their work. Only people who were born in the present but actually live in earlier times — women, the rural population, Orientals (including the Japanese) — as well as people with mutilated brains, such as necktie and wallpaper designers, are capable of creating new ornamentation of equal quality to the old.

The inability of our culture to create new ornament is a sign of its greatness. The evolution of humanity goes hand in hand with the disappearance of ornamentation from objects of everyday use. Whatever our applied artists, prompted by the survival instinct, may say, for people of culture a face without a tattoo is more beautiful than one with a tattoo, even if it has been designed by Kolo Moser[2] himself. And people of culture also want not only their skin but also their book bindings and bedside tables protected from the Indian ornamental frenzy of these state-appointed cultural barbarians.

Ornament that does not arise organically from the human soul, as it did with the old masters and still does with the modern Oriental, is worthless. Worthless, a waste of labor and materials. And its worthlessness is increasing daily. Today household goods which only five years ago *appeared* valuable to their purchasers have difficulty reaching even a tenth of their original price in the auction rooms. And make no mistake about it, those objects which are currently being produced in today's uncultured — that is anachronistic, unmodern — style will suffer the same fate in a few years' time.

Our goal should be to create works of lasting value. I do not have the privilege of sowing the seeds of my teaching in the hearts of the young generation and since I do not belong to any clique, I do not have the opportunity of participating in exhibitions. Therefore I invite anyone who is interested in how to go about producing interior design of lasting value to accompany me on a tour of apartments which were created under my direction.

People who say we should go back to the old styles are right — as long as they consider the products of the ornamental schools as modern. But a truly modern style of joinery and cabinetmaking will perhaps make them change their minds. One aim of these tours is to halt the relapse into a mishmash of old styles which has already become widespread. I will, I know, be accused of self-advertisement. Perhaps I can meet the accusation by pointing out that the apartments on which I collaborated have never appeared in art magazines and that it was never my habit to cackle whenever I laid an egg.

In order to protect the owners, who have so unselfishly agreed to open their homes, from too many and too importunate visitors, I have set a fee of twenty crowns for the two guided tours. Tickets can be obtained from Goldman & Salatsch in the Graben and the new retail outlet of Steiner's artificial flower factory in Kärntnerstraße. Each ticket is for two people, the proceeds going to the charity of the purchaser's choice.

My main hope is that those whose profession it is to create our interiors will take part in these guided tours — that is joiners, decorators and interior designers. One group is excluded: architects.

Do not think it is the plagiarists among them I fear. On the contrary, I would be delighted if every architect were to work along the same lines as I do. But they won't. They will only misunderstand me, just as they misunderstood my Café Museum. Ever since the café was opened, all apartments have been as bare as a café. In those days — it was the time of green, red, violet and gray wood stain, it was the time when every piece of furniture had to be forced into some circular shape, or huge circular arches made of laths spanned the room (may I remind you that Josef Hoffmann's premises for Apollo Candles and my Café Museum were done at the same time) — one at least had a sense of something that could, if you insist, be called "applied art." Since then, however, the decoration for vases and fruit bowls has been based on sewer gratings. That was not what I intended. If I hadn't done the Café Museum then, the whole decorative trend of Olbrich, van der Velde[3] and Hoffmann would have collapsed from over-ornamentation. My café showed them new but mistaken ways and I do not want to send them up yet another garden path. Our culture has a right to be left in peace by the experimenters for a while.

I hope as many as possible will come and discover what I really intended.

DAY ONE

1st district: Graben, at the junction with Naglergasse: Goldman & Salatsch store.

The premises were divided in two by a transverse arch. The arch was clad with huge brass and cut glass lamps, snakewood. Sprayed plaster.

1st district: 1 Naglergasse, 4th floor, Herr A.'s dining room.
(No elevator, entrance via Goldman & Salatsch.)
Brown-stained, varnished oak, fireplace *verde anticho*, Greece.

1st district: 33 Kärntnerstraße, Sigmund Steiner's store.
The doorway in brass and Skyros marble (Greece). The largest curved windowpanes in Vienna. Interior: a mirror set into the wall makes the small shop appear twice as large as it is. To complete the illusion the ceiling was divided by beams and the wall below the mirror was curtained. East Indian satinwood.

1st district: 6 Falkestraße (by the Stubentor), Herr W.'s music room. 3rd floor (elevator).
The vestibule uses old furniture painted white. The music room needs space for a quartet and seating for as large an audience as possible, therefore benches that can be placed across

the window and the door to the vestibule. The family are friendly with Wilhelm Unger and in places woodwork by him has been let into the wall covering. Genuine Japanese wallpaper; mahogany. A small table for coins by Miss Unger (Hoffmann school).

4th district: 19 Wohllebengasse, on the corner with Alleegasse. 2nd floor. Herr T.'s apartment. No elevator.

Vestibule not by me. Smoking room in mahogany, using existing furniture. Party wall at an angle, therefore a sideboard with many corners which create an optical illusion to mask the crooked wall. The oval table for the same reason. Family has a lot of old silver and porcelain, therefore the number of sideboards. Cherrywood. Wife's bedroom in maple.

4th district; 2 Schleifmühlgasse, Paulanerhof, 5th floor (elevator).

Herr W.'s dining room in dark-stained alder. Use of an old chest of drawers from the Maria Theresa period.

1st district: 13 Opernring, 3rd floor. Herr L.'s dining room (no elevator).

Originally two adjoining rooms, one large, one small; because of the cross beam a piece of the partition wall was left. The cross beam was clad with mahogany and, for the sake of symmetry, this cladding was repeated, thus creating a ceiling with wooden beams. Walls mahogany with 60 cm high x 240 cm wide pyramid grain (rare). Chair covered in pigskin. Window embrasure cladding *pavonazzo forno* (Italian marble). New sash windows with blinds of Teneriffe lace. The curtain is a piece of old peasant cloth from Bolzano (silk).

1st district: 15 Elisabethstraße, 5th floor. Herr S.'s smoking room.

Two adjoining rooms, the smaller one an irregular shape, were knocked together. Owner an amateur photographer. Dark room. The shape of the fireplace conceals the crooked party wall.

Handblocked English wallpaper. Natural oak (as for office furniture). Despite that, the old black upright piano fits in well. Bedroom in maple.

1st district: 13 Nibelungengasse, 2nd floor. Herr K.'s apartment (no elevator).

Owner moved in, bringing Portois & Fix furniture. Many alterations to improve the apartment. Window onto stairwell enlarged. (Note the original size on the 1st floor.) Part of the bathroom used for access to the new vestibule and dining room. New: vestibule in white paint with yellow plaster sprayed on. Room off dining room, half inglenook, half conservatory. Skyros marble. Donatello frieze.

DAY TWO

8th district: 24 Wickenburggasse, mezzanine. Dr. T.'s apartment.

Dining room in cherrywood, consulting room in mahogany, bedroom in *batiste rayée* (fabric for ladies' blouses). After my wife's bedroom, which appeared in the magazine *Kunst*.

9th district: 22 Alserstraße, 2nd floor. Dr. S.'s apartment (no elevator).

Vestibule painted white, dining room oak with a brown stain, Japanese wallpaper of grass cloth (woven from grass), sitting room painted white, old fireplace.

9th district: 53 Alserstraße, 3rd floor. Dr. H.'s apartment (no elevator).

Dining room. Also intended to be used as a reception room for visitors. Ugly stove altered to accommodate a large clock. Old Italian trough (plaster cast) used as a planter. Dark-stained oak. Study unfinished, arranged so it can be enlarged. Bedroom in maple.

8th district: 68 Josefstädterstraße, in the courtyard.
At the entrance to the courtyard press the knob of the door handle.
Dining room of Fräulein Ella Hofer, formerly of the *Volkstheater*, now resident in New York. Originally the house of Imperial Counsellor Hanusch. Room completely lacking in proportion. Ceiling lowered by use of exposed beams. Irregularly shaped smaller room added to it. Fireplace *polcevere* with Donatello casts. White paint and cherrywood, green sprayed plaster. Two ordinary windows made into one large window. The old large mullion made the room dark as there was a covered balcony built on.

8th district: 73 Josefstädterstraße, 3rd floor. Dr. G.'s apartment, opposite the previous one (elevator).
Vestibule not by me. Dining room painted white with mahogany. Smoking room: the piano is missing. A good example of the beginning of my work on an interior as I only sketch out the broad outlines. Unfinished as the owner only moved in two weeks ago.

1st district: 4 Bellaria, 2nd floor. Herr F.'s apartment (elevator).
(The first of Otto Wagner's buildings.) Owner plays the cello and collects fine bindings. Wife a sculptor.
Dining room: the architect brought a Berlin room from his student days in Berlin. Light from one side only, from the courtyard, therefore can only be used in the evening. Walls, sideboards and fireplace of *pavonazzo* (Italy), Japanese wallpaper. Chairs, copies of the famous Chippendale ribbon-backed chair (mahogany). Wall fountain, Pompeian snake (from their honeymoon). Music room in cherrywood, fireplace *vert-vert* (Belgium). Smoking room mahogany. Fireplace Tyrolean onyx.
All the dining chairs after originals in the Austrian Museum.
All other chairs after English originals by F. O. Schmidt.
The elephant-trunk table is from the workshop of F. O.

Schmidt, following details given by Max Schmidt (execution and details by the foreman, Berka). Tiles on the table top by Bigot, Paris.

All other modern pieces and light fittings by me.

These interiors were done over the last eight years.

I would like to thank the owners for their cooperation.

I only undertake commissions from clients who feel a genuine need to have their interiors designed. Snobs are excluded. The rooms are not shown in art magazines and there will be no more guided tours.

Notes

1. The bourgeois style of the years following the Napoleonic period, characterized by an elegant simplicity (especially compared with the later nineteenth century), partly derived from the Empire style.

2. Koloman Moser, 1868-1918, was one of the leading *art nouveau* designers in Vienna; he was a member of the *Sezession* and co-founder of its retail outlet, the *Wiener Werkstätte*.

3. Henri Clemens van der Velde, 1863-1957, a Belgian architect and designer and one of the originators of the *art nouveau* style.

11. The Discovery of Vienna (1907)

The most beautiful interior of a building: St. Stephen's Cathedral. I'm not saying anything new? All the better. It cannot be repeated often enough: we have the most reverence-inspiring church interior in the world. It is not a dead inventory item we have taken over from our fathers. It tells us our history. Every generation has added to it, in their own language. Until ours, that is, for we do not have a language of our own to speak. For that reason this space is at its most magnificent when the additions of the last forty years are silent. At twilight, for example, when you can ignore the windows. Then the space seems to pour in on you so that . . . I see I can't express the effect it has on me. But perhaps each individual should observe the feeling they have when they come out onto the street after walking round the cathedral. It is stronger than after Beethoven's Fifth. But that takes half an hour, St. Stephen's only half a minute.

The most beautiful town house: the Palais Liechtenstein in Bankgasse.[1] It is so completely unViennese, not in the petty Viennese Baroque style. Others might see virtues in that abstruse pettiness; let others call Hildebrand[2] master. Here we hear the mighty voice of Rome, unadulterated, without the scratchy background noise of a German gramophone. Go from Minoritenplatz along Abraham a Sancta Clara Gasse and lift up your head at the portal of this building.

The most beautiful dying building: The War Ministry on Am Hof square. Have a good look at it, citizens of Vienna, for soon it will be gone. Everyone knows it is soon to come down, but no one has raised a hand to stop this act of vandalism. Make sure you fix the image in your mind now so you can keep it in your heart. This building sets the tone for the whole square. Without it Am Hof will not be Am Hof anymore.

The most beautiful new building: When a house in the central district is torn down, do not people tremble at the thought of the monstrosity that will occupy its site? I trembled too when the building on the corner of Kärntnerstraße and Himmelpfortgasse was pulled down last year. But what joy: a building appeared which fits in perfectly with the spirit of Kärntnerstraße, which seems like a continuation of the old style of the center of Vienna, modest, calm, refined. This building will not appear in the art magazines, it isn't considered "artistic" enough. Nor is it what people call modern, i.e., vulgar. But the builder of the house will be as impervious to the criticism of "old-fashioned" hurled at him by modern architects as the man who dresses correctly is to the same gibe from the lips of a provincial tailor's apprentice. I would like to express my thanks to the unknown person who commissioned this building.

The most beautiful walk: The Beethoven Walk in Heiligenstadt in early spring.

Notes

1. The masterpiece of the Italian architect, Domenico Martinelli, 1650-1718.

2. Johann Lukas von Hildebrandt, 1668-1745, is generally regarded as the major architect of the Austrian Baroque after Fischer von Erlach.

12. An Appeal to the Citizens of Vienna Written on the Day of Lueger's[1] Death (1910)

With Lueger the guardian spirit of the church of St. Charles has gone to his grave.

Charles VI's[2] idea that the church should form the culmination point of a great broad avenue stretching from the Schottentor via Josefsplatz to the Wieden lived on in him.

The building of the Ringstraße frustrated this idea.

The design and situation of the church, its extended façade, which is not justified by the ground plan and is in stark contrast to the sober interior, clearly show that the church was merely a pretext for the creation of a focal point for a street.

The old original idea could no longer be carried out. We are the last people to have the right to criticize the builders of the Ring. Have we ourselves not, with Riehl Avenue, abandoned an old plan of Maria Theresa, who by the wedge-shaped arrangement of buildings wanted to give later generations the opportunity of continuing Praterstraße into the heart of the city?

Lueger, and with him all men of understanding, wanted to give St. Charles's the setting it deserves, the setting it needs.

To set it off, St. Charles's needs large horizontal surfaces and lines. These can only be provided by a public building. The Viennese, however, think the public building should be outside the city.

It is probably only chance that the imperial museums were not built on the Schmelz.[3] Otherwise their site would now be occupied by apartment houses.

The man who safeguarded the concept behind St. Charles's, the man who had the power to protect the church and the city from the vandalism threatening them, has died.

There is nothing left to stop Viennese taste having its way and building the museum[4] on the Schmelz.

But on the site until now reserved for it, three apartment houses will be built.

And now my appeal to the inhabitants of Vienna: make a

donation towards a plaque.

I am making this appeal so that the middle of the three apartment houses can have a plaque attached on which will be carved for all eternity the names of those to whose unsparing efforts we owe these three apartment houses.

The donations do not have to be large, since there are so many people in Vienna and a plaque costs so little.

With each contribution the donor can name one man whose services in bringing about these three apartment houses deserve a memorial.

A selection will be made from among those names.

Those of you who have boldly spoken out for the idea of the three apartment houses will be able to look with pride on your names on the memorial plaque.

Notes

1. Karl Lueger, 1844-1910, founder of the Austrian Christian Social Party and mayor of Vienna from 1897 until his death, was largely responsible for the modernization of the city; he was also a political anti-Semite, famous for his statement, "I'm the one who decides who's a Jew."

2. 1685-1740, Holy Roman Emperor from 1711 until 1740.

3. The *Schmelz* was a piece of open ground beyond the outer city walls, now forming part of the 15th district. From 1847 onward it was used for parades and military exercises; after 1911 it was released for building. The Museum of Natural History and the Museum of Art ("the imperial museums") were built on the Ring, opposite the Hofburg.

4. A *Kaiser-Franz-Joseph-Stadtmuseum* (city museum) was planned to be built next to the Rathaus, later on the Schmelz. Both Otto Wagner and Loos submitted designs, but neither project was carried out.

13. Some Questions Regarding Viennese Architecture (1910)

There is something particular about the architectural character of a city. Each has its own. Things that are beautiful and charming in one can look hideous and repulsive in another. The bare brick of Danzig would lose all its beauty if it were transplanted to Vienna. Do not talk of the force of habit. There are very specific reasons why Danzig is a city of brick, Vienna a city of plaster rendering.

I do not want to go into these reasons here, proving them would take up a whole book. But not only materials, architectural forms are also bound to a place, to its soil and air. Danzig has high, steep roofs. All the inventive imagination of Danzig architects went into finding ways of dealing with these roofs. Not so in Vienna. Vienna also has roofs, but our architects ignored them. If you are out in the streets at night around Midsummer's Day and they are empty and moonlit, you would think you were walking through a different town. No longer having to watch out for other pedestrians, carriages and automobiles, we are amazed to see a wealth of detail the day hides from us. And then we see the roofs of Vienna, see them for the first time, and are amazed that we fail to notice them by day.

Viennese architects, however, leave the roof entirely to the carpenter. Their task goes as far as the cornice and no farther. Aristocratic town houses may well have an attic over the cornice, with vases and figures, but ordinary mortals do not bother with these.

Five minutes from the center of Vienna, after crossing the former glacis on which Ringstraße has been built, there were "roofs." The selfsame architects who drew up no designs for roofs in the city center, were full of invention when it came to roofs and cupolas for houses in the surrounding districts. I only mention this to prove that our old architects took account of the character of a place and did everything possible to avoid spoiling it.

What I object to in our present architects is that they deliberately ignore the character of a place. The buildings on

Ringstraße[1] did fit in with the style of the city center. If the Ring were to be built today what we would get would not be the Ringstraße but an architectural catastrophe.

When I look from the Opera towards Schwarzenbergplatz I am filled with the feeling, Yes, that is the Ring, that is Vienna. But farther on, at the Stubenring, the feeling I get is, Six stories high, but just as provincial as Mährisch-Ostrau.[2]

Is that because the buildings on the Stubenring are bad? Or those on the Kärntnerring good? Neither is the case. There are good and bad buildings on both stretches of the Ring, buildings by artists and buildings by Philistines. But both artists and Philistines have taken the architectural character of Vienna into account on the Kärntnerring, while neither did on the Stubenring.

What is characteristically Viennese is the façade culminating in a straight cornice without roofs, cupolas, oriel windows or other additions above. The building regulations allow up to twenty-five meters to the upper edge of the cornice. But property owners feel the roof space needs to be utilized for studios and other rooms that can be rented out, because land is expensive and taxes high. So it was for financial reasons that the old character of Viennese architecture was lost. I know of a way of bringing it back. Not, God forbid, with new laws, which would take away more of the owners' rights, but with a relaxation of building regulations: anyone who undertakes to put nothing, nothing at all, above the cornice will be granted permission for a seven-story building. Rather an honest high building than those with rooftop monstrosities in what one might call the "lean-to style." Then our city would have handsome, monumental lines once more and grand proportions. For centuries we have breathed in the Italian air blowing over the Alps and with it Italian grandeur and monumentality, which have entered our bloodstream and for which the inhabitants of Danzig quite rightly envy us.

And then there is the plaster. In materialistic times such as ours people have started to look down their noses at it, to be ashamed of it. As a result, our good old Viennese rendering has been abused and prostituted, is no longer allowed to be itself but has to imitate stone. For stone is expensive and plaster cheap. But materials are not expensive or cheap in themselves. Air is cheap down here and expensive on the moon. For God and the artist all materials are equal and equally valuable, and I believe people should look at the world through the eyes of God, the eyes of the artist.

Plaster is a skin, stone a structural element. Despite the similarity of chemical composition there is the greatest possible difference between them as far as artistic use is concerned. Plaster has more in common with leather, wall-coverings and gloss paints than with its cousin, limestone. When plaster is honestly used as a covering for the bare brick wall, it has no more need to be ashamed of its simple origins than a Tyrolean in *lederhosen* and bare knees in the Imperial Palace. But if they both insist on wearing white tie and tails, the man will feel unsure of himself and the plaster will suddenly realize it is a confidence trickster.

The Imperial Palace! Its very proximity is a touchstone for genuine and false. There is a piece of advice I give to people who lack confidence in their own taste. If you want to decide whether an object is good or bad ask yourself, would this object look out of place in the Palace or not? That is the acid test, a test that apparently tasteful objects such as Copenhagen porcelain, Galée glass and the products of the *Wiener Werkstätte* fail, while examples of the most appalling bad taste, such as the Doberman pinscher painted on metal, sitting up and begging to hold the poker and fire-tongs, come out quite well. The Doberman is right and the Copenhagen cat is wrong.

There was a commission for a new building near the Imperial Palace, business premises, modern business premises. The question was to create a structure that would provide a transition from the imperial residence via the palatial town house of a feudal magnate to Vienna's most elegant shopping street, the Kohlmarkt. The site originally designated by Professor Mayreder and the present head of planning and building control, Herr Goldemund, was enlarged. Not, it must be said, to the advantage of the square. An attempt was made to correct this error with a colonnade of cipollino monoliths, allowing the façade to be taken back three and a half meters on the ground floor and mezzanine. It was to be a non-aristocratic building, which means that the architecture stops at the cornice; the copper roof will soon be black, so that only night owls on Midsummer's Day will be aware of it. And the four upper stories are to be rendered in plaster. Any necessary decoration will be honestly done, by hand, as our old Baroque craftsmen did in those happy days when there were no building regulations, because each man had the laws written in his heart.

On the ground floor and mezzanine, however, where the businesses will have their premises, modern business life demands a modern solution. And quite rightly so. The old masters have left us no models for a modern business. Nor for electric lights. If they were to rise from their graves they would find a solution soon enough. Not in the style of the so-called modern school. Nor in the style of archaizing designers who stick china candles with electric bulbs onto old candlesticks. Their solutions would be new and quite different from the concepts of either of these two opposing camps.

This has been attempted. An attempt has been made to make the building harmonize with the Imperial Palace, the square and the city. If the attempt is successful, then we will be grateful to the head of building control, Herr Greil, for the artistic sensitivity he showed in allowing a liberal interpretation of rigid regulations. We will be grateful to the city manager, Herr Pfeifer. And we will be grateful to the collaborating architect, Ernst Epstein, whose outstanding organizational ability and wealth of technical expertise will only be fully appreciated after the completion of the building.[3]

Notes

1. Largely put up in the 1870s.

2. Today Ostrava in the Czech Republic.

3. Loos is here talking about the building he designed on Michaelerplatz, which is the subject of the articles, "My First House!" and "My Building on Michaelerplatz;" the article "Architecture" is also relevant.

14. My First Building! (1910)

I do not know how to thank the City Planning Office for the free advertising they gave me with the ban on continuing work on the façade. A long-preserved secret was revealed: a building I have designed is being built.

My first building! A building! At my advanced age I had not in my wildest dreams thought a building of mine would be built. After everything I had been through I was well aware that no one would be so insane as to commission a building from me. Or that it would be possible to get my design accepted by any planning authorities.

I have had experience in dealing with them. I was entrusted with the honorable task of erecting a porter's lodge on the beautiful banks of Lake Geneva. There were many stones lying around on the lakeside and since the people who lived beside the lake had all built their houses of them, I decided to do the same. In the first place it would be cheap, which would be reflected in my fee — I would be paid much less — and in the second place transport would be easier. As a matter of principle I am against people having to do too much work, myself included.

So I was all unsuspecting when, like a bolt from the blue, I received a summons from the planning authorities, who asked me what I, a foreigner, thought I was doing desecrating the beauty of Lake Geneva. The house was much too plain. Where was the ornamentation? My mild objection that on calm days the lake itself was smooth and unornamented and still people found it quite nice was brushed aside. I was given a certificate stating that it was forbidden to build such a house for reason of its simplicity and therefore ugliness. Overjoyed, I made my way home.

Yes, overjoyed! Is there any other architect in the whole universe who has it in black and white from the authorities that he is an artist? We all like to think we are, but people don't always believe us. Some believe it of this architect, some of that, but in the majority of cases, no one at all believes it. Now everyone, even I, had to believe it of me. I was banned, banned by the authorities like Frank Wedekind or Arnold Schoenberg.[1]

Or rather, as Schoenberg would be banned if the authorities could read the thoughts behind his notes.

I was conscious of the fact that I was an artist. I had vaguely suspected this before, but now I had a certificate from the authorities to prove it, and as a good citizen I only believe things bearing an official stamp. But this consciousness was dearly bought. Someone, perhaps myself, let it slip and word got round so that no one wanted anything to do with such a dangerous person, which is what an artist always is. Not that I was without work, oh no. Anyone who had 1,000 crowns, but needed an interior that looked like 5,000 crowns, came to me. I became a specialist at that. People, however, who had 5,000 crowns and wanted a bedside table for it that looked like 1,000 crowns went to another architect. Since the first category is much more numerous than the second, I had quite enough to keep me occupied.

Then one day an unfortunate man came to me to commission the plans for a building. It was my tailor. This honest gentleman — actually two honest gentlemen — had supplied me with suits, year in, year out, and patiently sent a bill every January 1 which, I have to admit, never grew any smaller. Despite the violent protestations of my two patrons, I still cannot entirely free myself of the suspicion that they bestowed this prestigious commission on me in order at least to reduce the bill somewhat. The architect, you see, receives an honorarium, but the fine-sounding name is no guarantee it won't be set off against unpaid bills.

I warned the two honest gentlemen to beware of me. In vain. They were determined to reduce my outstanding bill — sorry, to commission the building from an officially certificated artist. I asked them if they were sure, as hitherto respectable citizens, they wanted the authorities on their backs. They were sure.

Everything happened as I had predicted. Fortunately the head of building control, Herr Greil, appeared at the last moment to wave away the constable who who had already been sent to stick the miscreants in the municipal lockup. The authorities, thank

God, always have higher authorities upon their backs to bite 'em.

The building will soon be finished. What will happen about my suits, I don't yet know. What I do know is that my clients never want to build another shop. I'll just have to look for another tailor. And if, when I find him, he turns out to be as intrepid as my present clothing suppliers, my second building will be going up in ten years' time.

Notes

1. Frank Wedekind, 1864-1918, a German cabaret performer and dramatist probably best known for the plays on which Alban Berg based his opera *Lulu*; was imprisoned in 1899 for insulting the crown. Many of Schoenberg's early works aroused a violently hostile reaction in the audience.

15. Architecture (1910)

May I take you to the shores of a mountain lake? The sky is blue, the water green and everywhere is profound tranquillity. The clouds and mountains are mirrored in the lake, the houses, farms and chapels as well. They do not look as if they were fashioned by man, it is as if they came straight from God's workshop, like the mountains and trees, the clouds and the blue sky. And everything exudes an air of beauty and peace . . .

But what is this? A discordant note in the tranquillity. Like an unnecessary screech. Among the locals' houses, that were not built by them, but by God, stands a villa. The creation of an architect. Whether a good or bad architect, I don't know. All I know is that the tranquillity, peace and beauty have vanished.

Before God there are no good or bad architects, in His presence all architects are equal. In the cities, in the presence of Belial, there are subtle nuances, as is the nature of vice. And therefore I ask, why is it that any architect, good or bad, desecrates the lake.

The farmer doesn't. Nor does the engineer who builds a railway along the shore or scores deep furrows in its clear surface with his ship. They go about things in a different way. The farmer marks out the site for his new house in the green meadow and digs out the trenches for the foundations. Then the mason appears. If there is clay in the area there will be a brickworks delivering bricks. If not, then he can use the stone from the shores of the lake. And while the mason is laying brick upon brick, stone upon stone, the carpenter arrives and sets up his tools. His ax rings out merrily. He is making the roof. What kind of roof? A beautiful or an ugly one? He has no idea. It's just a roof.

And then the joiner measures up the doors and windows, and all the other craftsmen come and measure up and go back to their workshops and work. Finally the farmer mixes up a large tub of whitewash and makes the house nice and white. He cleans the brush and puts it away. He'll need it again next Easter.

His intention was to erect a house for himself and his family, or for his animals, and that is what he has done. Just as his neighbor or his great-greatgrandfather did. Just as every animal does when it is guided by instinct. Is the house beautiful? Yes, just as beautiful as a rose or a thistle, as a horse or a cow.

And I repeat my question: why is it that the architect, no matter whether good or bad, desecrates the lake? Like almost all city dwellers, the architect lacks culture. He lacks the sure touch of the farmer, who does possess culture. The city dweller is rootless.

What I call culture is that balance between our physical, mental and spiritual being which alone can guarantee sensible thought and action.

I intend to give a lecture soon entitled, "Why do the Papuans have a culture and the Germans not?"

Until now there has been no period of non-culture in the history of mankind. This was reserved for the urban society of the second half of the nineteenth century. Until then culture developed in a steady flow. People responded to the demands of the moment and looked neither forward nor back.

Then the false prophets appeared, saying, "How ugly and joyless are our lives!" And they gathered together everything from all cultures, set it up in museums and said, "See, that is Beauty. You, however, were wallowing in ugliness."

So then there came household goods decorated with columns and cornices, like houses, there came silks and satins. Then, above all, there came ornamentation. And since the craftsman, as a man of modern culture, was incapable of designing ornamentation, schools were set up in which healthy young people were gradually warped until they were capable of it. Just as in China children are put into a vase and fed for years until they burst out in all their monstrous deformity. Like their Chinese counterparts, these deformed mental monstrosities were duly marveled at and had no difficulty earning a living, thanks to their deformity.

At that time there was no one to call out, "Stop and think. The path of culture leads *away* from ornamentation to unadorned plainness." The evolution of culture is synonymous with the removal of ornamentation from objects of everyday use. The Papuan covers everything he can lay his hands on with ornament, from his face and body to his bow and canoe.

But today tattoos are a sign of degeneracy and only seen on criminals and degenerate aristocrats. For people of culture, in contrast to the Papuans, a face without tattoos is more beautiful than one with tattoos, even if they had been designed by Michelangelo or Kolo Moser. The nineteenth-century person wants not only his face but also his suitcase, his clothes, his household goods and his house protected from these artificially generated Papuans. Gothic art? We are more advanced than the people of that period. The Renaissance? We are more advanced. We have become more sensitive, more refined. We lack the robust nerves necessary to drink out of an ivory tankard with a battle of the Amazons carved on it. Old techniques have vanished? The Lord be praised. We have been given Beethoven's music of the spheres in exchange. Our temples are no longer painted blue, red, green and white like the Parthenon, we have learned to appreciate the beauty of bare stone.

But, as I said, at that time there was no one around to remind people of this, and the enemies of our culture, those who sang the praises of foreign cultures, had it all their own way. They were, moreover, wrong. They had misunderstood earlier epochs. Since only those objects were kept which, thanks to their pointless ornamentation, were of less practical use and therefore did not wear out, only objects *with* ornamentation have come down to us. Consequently people assumed that in the past all objects had ornamentation. Also, it was easy to use ornamentation to classify objects by age and origin and cataloguing was — amongst other things — one of the most edifying pastimes of those goddamned times.

All this was beyond the honest craftsman. On one and the same day he was supposed to make everything that had been made throughout history in all nations and produce new inventions as well. But these things were the expressions of their culture and were produced by the craftsmen in the same way as the farmer builds his house. The craftsman of the present worked in the same way as the craftsman of the past. A contemporary of Goethe was no longer capable of making ornament. Therefore the warped product of the schools was brought in and the craftsman placed under his tutelage.

The mason and the master builder were also placed under tutelage. The master builder just built houses and that was called building in the style of his own times. The one who took control was the man who could build in the style of every past age, the man who had lost contact with his own times, the rootless man, the warped man, in a word, the architect.

Books meant little to the craftsman. The architect took everything from books. An abundance of works of reference provided everything and anything worth knowing. People have no idea of the way this mass of slick publishing ventures has poisoned our urban culture, the way it has prevented us from remembering who and what we are. It made no difference whether the architect had internalized the forms so that he could draw them from memory or whether he had to have the sourcebook open before him on the table while producing his "artistic creations," the effect was always the same: an abomination. And there was no end to the abomination. Everyone was desperate to see their things perpetuated in new publications and a large number of architectural periodicals appeared to satisfy the vanity of architects. And so it has remained to the present day.

There is another reason why the architect has ousted the craftsman. He has learned draftsmanship, and since that is all he has learnt, he is good at it. The craftsman is not. He has a heavy hand. The plans of the old master builders are clumsy, any student of building can do *that* better, not to mention the so-called "fluent hand" so keenly sought and handsomely paid by every firm of architects.

The architect has reduced the noble art of building to a graphic art. The one who receives the most commissions is not the one who can build best but the one whose work looks best on paper. There is a world of difference between the two.

If we were to range the arts in a row starting with the graphic arts, we will see that there are connections from them to painting. From there we can continue through colored sculpture to sculpture proper and from there to architecture. The graphic arts and architecture are polar opposites, at either end of the row.

The best draftsman can be a poor architect, the best architect a poor draftsman. Nowadays those entering architecture are expected to show a talent for graphic art. All our new architecture has been created on the drawing board, these drawings then being exhibited three-dimensionally, like paintings in a waxworks.

But for the old master builders the drawing was merely a means of communicating with the craftsmen who carried out the work. Just as a poet has to communicate through writing. However, we are not so totally devoid of culture as to get a boy to take up poetry just because he has a calligraphic hand.

It is a well-known fact that any work of art obeys such powerful inner laws that it can only be carried out in that one form.

A novel that can be made into a good drama is poor both as a novel and a drama. How much more starkly, then, does this come out when we take two different arts, even if there are points of contact between them. A painting that can be represented as a waxworks group is a bad painting. A presentable Tyrolean can be seen at Kastan's waxworks, but not a sunrise by Monet or an engraving by Whistler. What is really terrible, however, is to see an architectural drawing, which, given the medium, one has to accept as an example of graphic art — and there are genuine graphic artists among the architects — carried out in stone, iron and glass. The sign that a building arises from a genuine feel for architecture is that it makes no impression as a two-dimensional representation. If I could erase the most powerful architectural statement, the Pitti Palace, from people's memory and enter it for a competition, drawn by the best draftsman, the adjudicators would have me put away in a lunatic asylum.

As things are then, the "fluent hand" holds sway. Architectural forms are no longer created by the craftsman's tools, but
by the pencil. From the elevation of a building, from the manner
of a piece of ornamentation, one can tell whether the architect
was using a no. 1 or a no. 5 pencil. And what terrible havoc the
compass has wreaked on our taste! Since architects have taken up
the ruling pen, architectural drawings have come out in a rash of
little squares and no window embrasure, no marble slab is unin-
fected. The tiniest details are drawn in on a scale of 1:100 and the
bricklayer and stonemason have to chip out or build up the
graphic nonsense by the sweat of their brow. If the draftsman
happens to have colored ink in his pen, then the gilder has to be
called in.

But I repeat: a true building makes no impression as a picture,
reduced to two dimensions. It is my greatest pride that the
interiors I have created are completely lacking in effect when
photographed; that the people who live in them do not recognize
their own apartments from the photographs, just as the owners
of a Monet would not recognize it at Kastan's waxworks. The
honor of seeing my works published in the various architectural
journals is something I have had to do without. I am denied the
satisfaction of my vanity.

Does this perhaps mean I am working in a vacuum? Nothing
of mine is known. But this is where the power of my ideas and
the rightness of my teachings become apparent. I, the un-
published architect, I, the man working in a vacuum, am the only
one among thousands who has real influence. I can give an
example. When I finally had the chance to create an interior — it
was hard enough since, as I have said, my kind of work *cannot* be
represented graphically — the response was very hostile. That
was twelve years ago when I did the Café Museum in Vienna.
The architects called it "Café Anarchism." But my Café Museum
still stands today while all the modern joinery of the thousands
of others has long since been consigned to the junk room. Or
they are ashamed of it. That the Café Museum has had more

influence on modern joinery work than all previous projects put together can be proved by a quick glance at the 1899 volume of the Munich journal, *Dekorative Kunst*, where this interior was reproduced, presumably due to a mistake by the editor. But these two photographic illustrations had no influence; at the time they were completely ignored. Thus, as you can see, it is only the power of the example that has influence. It was by this power that the influence of the old craftsmen spread more rapidly to the most distant corners of the earth despite or, rather, because of the fact that there was no postal service, no telegraph or newspapers.

The second half of the nineteenth century was filled with the sound of the false prophets, men without culture, crying, "We have no architectural style!" How wrong, how incorrect. That was the very time that had a more distinct style, one that differed more distinctly from the preceding period, a change unparalleled in cultural history. Since, however, these false prophets could only recognize a product by the varying ornamentation, this orna-mentation became a fetish for them and they substituted it for the real thing, calling it "style." Style we already had, but no ornamentation. If I were to chip off all the ornamentation from our old and new buildings, leaving only the bare walls, I would certainly find it difficult to distinguish fifteenth-century from seventeenth-century buildings. But even the man in the street would recognize those of the nineteenth century at a glance. We had no ornamentation and they moaned that we had no style. So they kept on copying ornaments from the past until even they found it ridiculous, so when they had gone as far as they could go in that direction, they started inventing new ornaments. That is, they had sunk to such a low cultural level that they were able to do that. And now they congratulate themselves on having created the style of the twentieth century.

But that is not the style of the twentieth century. There are many objects which show the style of the twentieth century in its pure form, and these are objects produced by craftsmen who were not working under the tutelage of one of the warped graduates of the schools. First and foremost they are the tailors, they are the shoemakers, the makers of bags and saddles, carriages and instruments and all those who avoided the fate of being uprooted from our culture because their craft seemed too ordinary to the false prophets to be worth reforming. What good fortune! From such scraps as the architects left me I was able, twelve years ago, to reconstruct modern joinery work, the joinery we would have if the architects had never stuck their noses in a joiner's workshop. I did not approach the task like an artist, giving free rein to his creative imagination (as they doubtless put it in artistic circles). No. I went to the workshops, as timid as an apprentice, looked up respectfully to the man in the blue apron, and asked him to share his secrets with me. For many a piece of workshop tradition still lay there, bashfully hidden from the eyes of the architects. And when they realized what I wanted, when they saw I was not one of those who would deface their beloved wood with his drawing-board fantasies, when they saw I had no intention of defiling the noble color of their revered material with green or violet stains, they glowed with craftsman's pride, revealed their carefully concealed tradition and gave vent to their hatred of their oppressors. I found modern paneling in the cladding of the old lavatory water tanks, I found a modern solution for the problem of corners in the chests for silver cutlery, I found locks and metal fittings on suitcases and pianos. And I found out the most important thing, namely that the style of 1900 only differs from the style of 1800 to the same extent as the tail coat of 1900 differs from that of 1800.

By not very much, that is. The one was made of blue cloth and had gold buttons, the other is of black cloth and has black buttons. The black coat is in the style of our times, that no one can deny. In their arrogance the warped graduates of the schools had not bothered to reform our clothing. They were all serious-minded and felt it beneath their dignity to waste their time on such things. That is why our clothing has remained in the style of our times. The invention of ornament was the only activity deemed worthy of such dignified, serious-minded men.

When I finally received a commission for a building, I said to myself, "In its external appearance a building can at most have changed as much as a tail coat. By not very much, that is." And I saw how our ancestors built and I saw how, century by century, year by year, they had freed themselves from ornamentation. So I had to go back to the point where the chain had broken. One thing I did know: in order to continue the line of this development I had to be appreciably simpler. I had to replace the gold buttons with black ones. The building had to look unobtrusive. Had I not once said, modern dress is that which draws least attention to itself. It sounded paradoxical, but there were good honest people who carefully collected it, like so many of my paradoxical ideas, and put it into print again. It happened so often people eventually accepted it as true.

But as far as inconspicuousness was concerned, there was one thing I had not taken into account. What was true of clothing was not true of architecture. If our warped graduates had left architecture in peace and reformed our clothing along the lines of old theater costumes or the *Sezession*, then presumably the reverse would have been the case.

Just try to visualize it. Everyone is wearing clothes from some past age or other, or from some distant, imaginary future. You see men from the mists of antiquity, women with piled-up hair-styles and farthingales, exquisite gentlemen in Burgundian hose. And among them will be a few roguish moderns in purple pumps and apple-green silk jerkins with appliqué work by Professor Walter Scherbel. And now a man in a plain overcoat appears among them. Would he not arouse attention? Even more, would he not cause offense? And would not the police come, whose job it is to remove anything and anyone that causes a public nuisance?

It is the reverse that is the case, however. Our clothes are right, the fancy-dress ball is in architecture. My building (the so-called "Loos Building" on Michaelerplatz in Vienna, which was built in the same year as this article was written) really caused offense and the authorities were on the spot in no time at all. That kind of thing was all right in the privacy of someone's home, but not out in the street.

Some doubts will have crept in during these last remarks, doubts about the validity of comparing tailoring and architecture. Architecture is an art, after all. I grant you that, for the moment anyway. But have you never noticed the remarkable correspondence between people's appearance and that of buildings? Does not the Gothic style go with the extravagantly tagged and scalloped dress of the times? The Baroque with the full-bottomed wig? But do our modern buildings go with our dress? People are afraid of uniformity? Were not the old buildings of the same period and the same country uniform? So uniform we can sort them out according to styles and countries, nations and cities. This neurotic vanity, this vain neurosis of having to do things differently from one's fellow craftsmen at all costs was unknown to the old artisans. Tradition determined the forms. And it was not forms that changed it, but the craftsmen, who found conditions arose under which they could not remain true to the fixed, hallowed, traditional form. New tasks changed the forms and thus the rules were broken, new forms arose. But the *people* of those times were in harmony with the *architecture* of their times. The new building that had gone up pleased everyone. Today, however, most buildings only please two people: the architect and his client.

A building should please everyone, unlike a work of art, which does not have to please anyone. A work of art is a private matter for the artist, a building is not. A work of art is brought into the world without there being a need for it, a building meets a need. A work of art has no responsibility to anyone, a building to everyone. The aim of a work of art is to make us feel uncomfortable, a building is there for our comfort. A work of art is revolutionary, a building conservative. A work of art is concerned with the future and directs us along new paths, a building is concerned with the present. We love anything that adds to our comfort, we hate anything that tries to pester us into abandoning our established and secure position. We love buildings and hate art.

So the building has nothing to do with art and architecture is not one of the arts? That is so.

Only a tiny part of architecture comes under art: monuments. Everything else, everything that serves some practical purpose, should be ejected from the realm of art.

Only when we have got rid of the great misunderstanding that art is something that can be harnessed to a practical purpose, only when the fallacious catchphrase "applied art" has disappeared from the vocabulary of all nations, will we have the architecture of our times. The artist has only himself to consider, the architect society as a whole. But combining art and craft has done immeasurable harm to both, and to mankind. We no longer know what art is. In blind fury we persecute the artist and prevent the creation of works of art. Hourly we commit the great sin, the sin that cannot be forgiven, the sin against the holy spirit. Murder, robbery, everything can be forgiven. But all those ninth symphonies, the creation of which mankind in its blindness has prevented through its persecution of artists — no, not even that, through its sins of omission — will not be forgiven us. It is thwarting God's design.

Mankind no longer knows what art is. "Art in the service of commerce" was the title of a recent exhibition in Munich and there was no one to score out the offending words. And no one laughs at that splendid expression "applied art."

But to anyone who knows that art is there to lead mankind on and on, higher and higher, to make us more and more like gods, combining art with a material function is a profanation of the great goddess. People do not leave the artist free to do as he thinks fit because they are not in awe of him, and craftwork cannot develop freely because of the weight of aesthetic expectations we place on it. It is not the business of the artist to have the majority of his contemporaries behind him, his realm is the future.

Since there are buildings in good and bad taste, people assume the former are designed by artists, the latter by non-artists. But building in good taste should be just as much a matter of course as not putting your knife in your mouth or cleaning your teeth in the morning. People are here confusing art and culture. Can you show me one piece of bad taste from past times, that is from a cultured age? The buildings of the least master mason in a provincial town were in good taste. Of course there were great masters and lesser masters. Thanks to their profound knowledge, the great masters were in closer contact with the world spirit than the others.

Architecture arouses moods in people, so the task of the architect is to give these moods concrete expression. A room must look cozy, a house comfortable to live in. To secret vice the law courts must seem to make a threatening gesture. A bank must say, "Here your money is safe in the hands of honest people."

An architect can only achieve this by going back to those buildings of the past which aroused these moods in people. For the Chinese, white is the color of mourning, for us black. Therefore our architects would find it impossible to create cheerful moods with black paint.

If we were to come across a mound in the woods, six foot long by three foot wide, with the soil piled up in a pyramid, a somber mood would come over us and a voice inside us would say, "There is someone buried here." *That is architecture.*

Our culture is founded on the recognition of the all-transcending greatness of classical antiquity. Our manner of thinking and feeling we have adopted from the Romans, who taught us to think socially and discipline our emotions.

It is not mere chance that the Romans were incapable of inventing a new order of columns, a new ornament. The Greeks, who invented the moldings, were individualists, scarcely able to govern their own cities. The Romans invented social organization and governed the whole world. The Greeks applied their imagination to the elevation, which is individual, the Romans to the ground plan, which is general. The Romans were more advanced than the Greeks, we are more advanced than the Romans. The great masters of architecture believed they built like the Romans. They were mistaken. Period, place, climate frustrated their plans. But whenever lesser architects tried to ignore tradition, whenever ornamentation became rampant, a master would appear to remind us of the Roman origins of our architecture and pick up the thread again.

The last great master arose at the beginning of the nineteenth century: Schinkel. We have forgotten him. But the light of this great figure will fall on future generations of architects.

16. Otto Wagner (1911)

Göttweihgasse consists of only two buildings. A few years ago I had business in the one in which the Telegraph Office is housed. I was struck the moment I entered the lobby, but by the time I was going up the stairs I was confused. The building was certainly quite old, had been built around the middle of the nineteenth century, but this lobby, this staircase could only be the work of one man: Otto Wagner.

Shaking my head, I had a good look at the building from outside. I knew it well, but now I saw it with new eyes. Yes, from outside as well there was a touch of Otto Wagner about it. It has always been a source of pleasure to me to rediscover the authors of the old apartment houses who have mostly been forgotten. I find it easy, for example, to pick out the buildings Hetzendorf von Hohenberg, who built the Palais Pallavicini on Josefsplatz, put up in Vienna around the end of the 18th century. One by one I also identified Otto Wagner's works, and he always confirmed that I was right. The magnificent Café Opera, for example, one of the most exquisite architectural creations of the early 1860s, although we have lost the ability to appreciate its subtleties. So I went to see Otto Wagner again, to inform him of my latest archaeological find.

No, the building was not by him. It was too old for that. But there was a connection. Pure chance. It was the house where his parents lived, the house where he had spent his childhood.

We can thank chance that it was in this particular building that on 13 July 1841 a son was born to Rudolf Simon Wagner, notary to the Royal Hungarian Court, and his wife, Susanne Wagner, née von Helfferstorffer. For at that time the house was modern and it is unusually spacious. These are the childhood memories in which the work of this great man and great architect is steeped. For fifty years the sober severity of the building has exercised a restraining influence on his exuberant imagination. It is true, of course, that he was fortunate in his studies, and that also played its part. After graduating from the Academy in Vienna, where he was taught by van der Nüll,[1] he went to the

Royal Academy of Building in Berlin. In Vienna they took what
they needed where they found it. Orders of columns, moldings
and ornaments from two millennia were gathered together and
used in the one building. It was a recipe their mentor could use
to design the Opera and the Palais Larisch, but the unrestrained
eclecticism was disastrous for his students. Berlin was a salutary
antidote. The shadow of Schinkel's greatness still lay on Berlin's
architects. There was a cool, somewhat narrow-minded classicism
at work there, but this narrow-mindedness never harmed Otto
Wagner. He was too robust, too Viennese for that. But he
benefited from the classical discipline.

He was fortunate enough to receive numerous commissions
while still young. No. 4, Bellaria is presumably his first independent project.[2] Of all his works it shows the strongest Berlin
influence; the two oriels are later additions. There followed
Danzer's *Orpheum*[3] with its basilica ceiling. He was also commissioned to do interiors, and here he revealed such a wealth of
imagination that, going through these rooms today, one is
amazed. One can hardly believe that, at the height of the Makart
age,[4] there was a man who, despite the old-fashioned details,
could achieve such surprisingly modern effects. These rooms —
I am thinking, for example, of Meyer's apartment on the
Embankment — are full of an imaginative power which I find
breathtaking. Here is a man who was struggling to express a
great, monumental idea, struggling with the smallness of the
building.

And now I come to the tragic part of the life of this great
imaginative artist. An architect capable of finding solutions for
the greatest large-scale public buildings of our times could not get
a commission for one. There was no competition he did not
enter. But Otto Wagner was an artist and therefore the first prize
was always denied him. When you look through his works you
feel like shedding tears of rage at the fact that these magnificent
ideas were not carried out, and at the designs that were preferred
to his. Everywhere mediocrity triumphed over the artist. Truly,
I would not like to have lived through such a life of disappoint-

ments. I would not have had the strength.

Even Wagner's opponents will be forced to agree with me if they look at the sketches, projects and executed designs which have been published by Schroll since 1891. His building for the Berlin *Reichstag*, his parliament for Budapest, his peace palace in The Hague never got off the drawing board. In the meantime he was allowed to let off steam on apartment houses.

Yes, to let off steam. There is much to be said against the two apartment houses in Stadiongasse,[5] but one has to take into account the frame of mind he was in. Like a caged lion killing a fly, he struck too hard. He struck the wrong chords, agreed, too powerful for an apartment house, but these chords are beautiful. The first house coming from the direction of the Ring has an entrance hall that fills you with awe, so majestic is it in its spaciousness. The sign, "No hawking or begging," is superfluous here, no beggar or hawker would dare to enter such a place. Everything is achieved through form, without costly materials. Again and again I have been deeply moved by the way Otto Wagner has sought to increase the effect of the perspective by his wedge-shaped disposition of the pillars. It is his struggle to achieve, in a small space, in a minor commission, the grand effect for which his contemporaries denied him the proper setting. Add to that the doubts he had to overcome, the sleepless nights spent wrestling with the question whether such a bold design would achieve its effect. This wedge-shaped arrangement of pillars is a stroke of genius for which alone his name deserves to be written in architecture's roll of honor.

One large-scale public commission was granted him, the platforms and imperial pavilion for the silver wedding celebrations of the Emperor and Empress.[6] Monumentality, if only for a day!

On the other hand, they did not bar him from building his own house.[7] This remarkable building stands in the valley of Hütteldorf. Remarkable in two respects. The house is unlike any other and therefore, despite its baroque ornamentation, a modern building. But even more remarkable is that fact that, despite its foreign look, it still has a deep-rooted connection with Viennese tradition: with Hetzendorf von Hohenberg's *gloriette* in Schönbrunn. One hundred years — and the architectural rebirth of Greece — separate them. While in Hohenberg's design the columns are combined with arches, a Roman concept, Wagner's villa has a horizontal Greek architrave. But the two side projections with the huge vases are present with, above them, elaborate cartouches inscribed with the two mottos that have dominated his life, *Sine arte, sine amore non est vita* and *Artis sola domina necessitas*.[8]

He received three further large-scale commissions: the *Länderbank* in Hohenstaufengasse, the Diana Baths and the synagogue in Budapest.[9]

The *Länderbank* is still done in a free interpretation of Renaissance style while the atrium of the Diana Baths already anticipates Wagner's later works. Very simple means were probably never used to greater effect. The delicacy of the molding on the whitewashed walls and the sparing use of brass for the light fittings and door handles produce a marvel of elegance and grandeur.

And now Wagner the thinker came to the fore. *Artis sola domina necessitas* was expounded in a brochure entitled *Moderne Architektur*. There followed the apartment houses in Heugasse, enclosing the Palais Hoyos, and the apartment house in Universitätsstraße.[10] In the former he tried articulating the structure horizontally, in the latter vertically. The latter in particular aroused a storm of outraged protest. *Hosenträgerhaus* ("supender house") was the mocking name given to it. Despite this, and presumably as a result of his large-scale project *Artibus*, a conceptual design for a group of buildings dedicated to all the arts which aroused the enthusiasm of his colleagues all over the world, in 1894 he was appointed professor at the Academy as successor to Hasemann.

He was commissioned to design the façades for the Vienna urban railway.[11] In that year came his break with both his own and the Viennese tradition, a break which I, personally, regret.

He deliberately moved away from the architectural language of antiquity and tried to speak in a language of his own. That was and remains a mistake. Even modern writers can express everything they have to say in the language they were brought up with. There is no need for Volapük. Otto Wagner made the mistake of becoming passionately involved in the Belgian efforts to invent new ornamentation.

My views on this are well known. Thirteen years ago I sent out a warning, expressing the opinion that we are no longer capable of inventing new ornamentation. (My enemies take this to mean I am opposed to all ornamentation, while all I oppose is any kind of imitation in materials.) Anyone who wants to decorate something should therefore use the old ornaments. I do not consider the invention of new ornamentation as a sign of strength but — in cultivated people — as a sign of degeneration. The Papuans can go on inventing new ornaments until they finally reach the stage when they are beyond ornament.

Otto Wagner is not a degenerate. I do not think I am giving away any secrets when I say that the flood of dreadful sunflowers, spirals, zigzag lines, tendrils and earthworms from the Wagner studios, with which the poor city was awash at that time, did not come from him, but from the associates gathered in his studio. I remember Leopold Bauer proudly telling us the seven parallel snakes that accompany passengers down the steps of Karlsplatz station — and whose heads are now fortunately being eaten away by mold — were the product of his imagination. Wagner accepted them, and that was not always for the good. Even if the master's strict design meant that these ornamental excesses only appeared as surface decoration, his students also worked on their own account, and in the interior of the premises of Apollo Candles[12] we have a sad example of what they produced.

But works on which his ornamentalists were not allowed to collaborate, such as the magnificent sluice for the Danube Canal at Nußdorf,[13] will last for all eternity.

As you can see, I do not think everything that has come from

Wagner's workshop is good. I am a supporter of tradition, Wagner denies it. And yet all of us, his friends and his opponents, have to admit, with pride, that the greatest living architect is an Austrian and lives in Vienna. The milestones in the development of architecture during the nineteenth century bear the names of Schinkel, Semper, Wagner. The world knows that; it is only in Vienna that not everyone is aware of it. The mistakes of the great are more important for the development of mankind than the virtues of lesser mortals. He has many years to go before he reaches the age of Michelangelo, which I am sure this youthful seventy-year-old will. I just hope that the city he lives in and the empire he belongs to will have the sense to make good use of these valuable years.

Notes

1. Eduard van der Nüll, 1812-1868, designed the Vienna Opera (with August Siccard von Siccardsburg).

2. 1869.

3. A vaudeville theater taken over by Eduard Danzer in 1872; it continued to be known by his name even under later owners.

4. Named after the painter Hans Makart, 1840-1885, whose huge historical canvases and sumptuous furnishings dominated the taste of the wealthy Viennese middle classes during much of the 1870s and 1880s.

5. 1882-83.

6. 1879.

7. Presumably the reference is to his first house, built in 1886-88; in 1912-13 he built another beside it.

8. Without art and without love there is no life; Necessity is the sole mistress of art.

9. The synagogue in 1871, the bank in 1883-84.

10. 1888.

11. 1894 onward.

12. By Josef Hoffmann, a pupil of Otto Wagner.

13. 1894-98

17. My Building on Michaelerplatz (1911)

When the menswear firm of Goldman & Salatsch decided to build new premises they invited eight architects to take part in a competition. I was to be the ninth. I was the only one to refuse. I know very well that the system of competitions is a cancer eating away at modern architecture. I know that the best architect never wins the prize; the project that is carried out is the one with the most immediate appeal. Competitions are appropriate for ladies' hair-styles and hats, though obviously five years later different entries would be chosen as the best. The same would happen with our architecture competitions, but by then it's too late. This means that an architect who is only five years ahead of his time has no chance in a competition.

So I said to Goldman & Salatsch, "I only work to commission. Let us agree on a contract." And I drew up a contract:

1. We commission Adolf Loos to provide plans for the building on the corner of Kohlmarkt and Herrengasse.

2. If someone else should produce a better ground plan than Adolf Loos, he will withdraw from the commission.

3. The decision on the ground plan is ours. There will be no discussion of the façade.

The point of the contract is clear. So far I have always rejected a commission if I knew there was someone who could do it better. The clients, I knew, were intelligent men who understood their business and I was quite happy to accept their judgment of what was good or bad. They must know what their business needs. They must know which ground plan is economical, which would facilitate the running of their business, which impede it. Lighting can be explained. A façade cannot be explained. There is only one person who knows the effect it will have: the one who conceived it. Neither drawings nor models can give the slightest idea of its real appearance. I know that Viennese property owners are not as lacking in taste as Viennese designers of façades. All the dreadful façades of recent years would have remained unbuilt if the clients had foreseen the effect.

The contract was signed and I got down to work.

Here I must acknowledge the great contribution one of the clients, Herr Leopold Goldman, made to working out the ground plan. It is thanks to his collaboration, thanks to his brilliant ideas, thanks to his business knowledge, which repeatedly crystallized in genuine innovations, that the ground plan developed as it did. And there is one other thing I must thank him for. He stood by me, unwaveringly, when the whole of Vienna seemed to be attacking the building, when people were saying, "The whole of Vienna has good taste, apart from Loos."

It was interesting to compare the other architects' plans with mine. Although central heating was stipulated, they all had the same thick internal walls, the only reason for which is to take the chimneys. The ground plans were all two-dimensional solutions whereas I believe an architect should work spatially, in three dimensions. That meant I had an advantage in the economy of space. A water closet does not need to be as high as a grand reception room. Giving each room the amount of height it needs and no more means one can build more economically. Secondly, it was striking that all of them made the the the main floor — the one above the ground floor which will house the shop and which is the reason the clients wanted their own building — the lowest. When houses were built in Vienna with the third floor the main one, that was made the highest. If someone in the eighteenth century had asked one of the great architects of the time to make the floor immediately above the ground floor the main one, he would have solved the problem straight away. Only lesser architects would have resisted the idea.

Even more remarkable was the number of courtyards. Building regulations quite rightly stipulate that a certain percentage of the area must be left as courtyard space. It is well known that a large courtyard gives a lot of light, a small one very little. Almost all the other entrants had arranged for three or four courtyards.

I also have to point out that the original building line, as proposed by Herr Goldemund when he was still in charge of the regulatory plan for the city, has been moved forward, much to

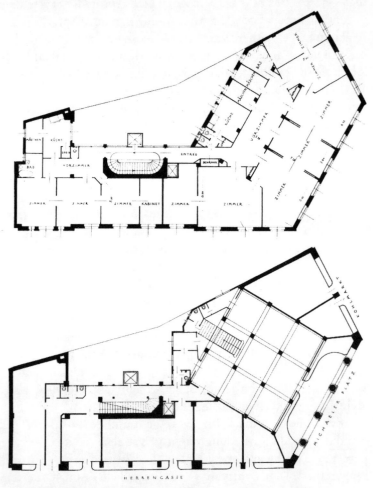

Building on Michaelerplatz: plans submitted with planning application.

the detriment of the square. Professor Ohmann, although himself an official in the building control department, refused to participate in the closed competition because he did not like the new line. In his opinion the correct line for the square should correspond to the church.[1] The idea in the regulatory plan was an oblique façade opposite the corner with Neumann's and the projects were designed accordingly. But the city council, to save themselves part of the sum for compulsory purchase, decreed that the façade should be brought forward by two meters. I considered that a disaster. True, my clients were delighted to have more space for their building, but despite that I went to see the director of the city building department and asked him to use his influence to have his original plan reinstated. The new line would make the front of the building so narrow it would look disproportionately high and dominate the church. Moving the building line forward would also make the main façade three meters narrower.

Seduced by the two obtuse angles, almost all the designs gave the corners corbeled turrets, a variation on Orendi's store. "Out you come," was the general motto, and I was saying, "Get back, get back." In my naïveté, I imagined that by pulling back on the ground floor and presenting the Viennese with so much valuable street space I would have earned the life-saving medal first class.

But there was another reason for pulling back. Everyone feels that large plate-glass windows would be out of place here. The whole square is dominated by the Hofburg, which creates a specific axis with the Michaelerkirche on one side. The new building will be its counterpart on the other. Both the closeness to the imperial palace as well as the parallel with the church demanded a modification of the plate-glass entrance. It has to be a store, but an exclusive store. I said to my clients, "You are tailors and your prices are between Rothberger's and Frank's. That must also be expressed in the building. Rothberger's have their windows on the street, nothing of Frank's can be seen on the street. You must come somewhere in between." They went along with me and opened up their most valuable space to the citizens of Vienna.

I asked them not to press me for details of the final design for the four upper stories for the moment. I still did not know what material would be available to me since I wanted to go to Greece to look for it. For the interim, Herr Epstein, the architect supervising the building, had drawn a simple façade for the four upper floors. I knew I would choose cipollino marble, but each block has different patterning and I wanted to know my stone first. That was the reason I put off the final decision on the four upper stories.

The effect of the the elevation was as I expected. The authorities were happy enough with the upper stories, but felt the lower ones were too plain. As one of the city officials put it, "The ground floor and mezzanine would be all right in a working-class district like Ottakring, but not in the city center."

I will say a little about the design of the façade. The main columns are 122 cm wide and 80 cm deep, the narrow columns 80 by 80. These gave me that mathematical rhythm without which there can be no architecture. In order to ensure that the building was not too heavily monumental, however, to show that a tailor, albeit an exclusive tailor, had his premises there, I made the windows English bow windows; in addition, the small panes ensured the interior would have an intimate feel to it. All these panes are 17.1 cm square, also supporting my mathematical rhythm. I felt proud that, when a teacher asked her pupils what they associated with the expression "the Loos Building," one answer was mathematics and a sonata. A reward for the many nights spent at my squared drawing board.

But these bow windows have two further functions. The first is economic. Although the strength of the 80-cm-thick walls is fully expressed, the fact that the windows curve out as far as the building line means that little space is lost. The second function is aesthetic. To make the space easier to rent out under Viennese conditions, the lower floors of the Kohlmarkt frontage have only two openings, two window axes. Above them I have three, three vertical lines of windows, corresponding to the arrangement of rooms. And now I found a solution of which I am very proud. The window axes of the ground floor and mezzanine do not correspond to those of the upper floors. A sharp division between the residential floors and the business premises in both material and treatment was intended and the lack of correspondence between the window axes reinforces this. The problem now was to find an aesthetic solution for this bold step.

There is an anecdote about Anton Bruckner in which he says to the students in his harmony class, "And now I come to the biggest mistake that can be made in music. It is such and such. Just be sure none of you make it. It is the worst thing of all. This mistake occurs just twice in the whole history of music, in Beethoven's sonata number so-and-so and in my second symphony."

It is the same here. If anyone can solve the mistake as I have done here, so that the effect on the naïve, unprejudiced observer is not unaesthetic, then he should go ahead and make it himself. The bow windows jutting out at less than forty-five degrees and divided up into equal squares divert the eye from the window axes and the inserted pillars do the rest. These inserted pillars, an old Viennese feature that appears to such magnificent effect in a similar arrangement in the garden portal of the Palais Liechtenstein in the Rossau[2] and was also used by Otto Wagner for the stations of the urban railroad, were criticized for not being load-bearing.

I would ignore this criticism, as it was made by a non-specialist who likes to play the art historian, but since the public in general assumes, because he comments on matters relating to static equilibrium, he is a qualified expert, I will have to teach him a public lesson. He has been so willing to learn from the articles I wrote in the *Neue Freie Presse* thirteen years ago that complete sentences from them flow from his pen and people keep asking me whether I have started writing under the pseudonym of Lux.[3] This pseudo-expert expressed his surprise that I of all people, the opponent of ornament, should make the blunder of employing ornamental pillars. Let us be clear about it:

a pillar is not an ornament but a load-bearing architectural element and I am fighting to stop it being turned into an ornament. Whether the building would still stand if the pillars were absent is my affair. I could have broken the whole wall up into pillars. The safety standards I work to are my business. You could take every second column away from the Parthenon and the building would remain standing. The window mullions in a dwelling house are unnecessarily broad for structural reasons. The aestheticist might criticize them, but not the structural engineer. Even when the pillars are only inserted later, if they are correctly wedged in they will be load-bearing in a few days, as the expert knows. The same is true of the large pillars. We were longing for them to come. The extremely strong wooden beams, which had to support the large aperture until the marble columns arrived, bent like candles under the immense load, sagging by eight centimeters, even though the calculation of forces indicated complete stability without the pillars. But a house is not a railway bridge that goes down when the train runs over it and then pops back up again.

From a structural point of view the pillars inserted at mezzanine level are probably unnecessary. But the ground floor demanded large window panes and these pillars help distribute the load and at the same time provide a bridge to the residential floors, telling the observer that the mezzanine houses not a department store, but an exclusive gentleman's outfitters that does not need large windows because they would be out of keeping with the intimate atmosphere of the business. They also reduce the wide span of the window since, with the low cornice height available, it was not possible to find a satisfactory aesthetic solution for this span. The weight of the cornice is transferred to these pillars which then transfer it via the horizontal beam to the side piers of the ground floor. This solution was usual in all nations for large spans in interiors where such pillars, set on consoles, transferred the weight of the ceiling to the surrounding wall.

So no blunder at all. Such misjudgments are irritating,

especially coming from the pen of a man who — anonymously — edits volumes of plans and illustrations which, under his full name, he fights against as a great danger to modern life and art. Long may he continue his fight.

For the way in which the non-specialist ought to judge this kind of thing he should follow the example of Raoul Auernheimer, who wrote in his article *Häusertod* (The Death of Buildings), "Whatever one thinks of Loos's building, at least it does not give the impression of a laughing heir. It clearly takes little pleasure in its modernity, it has a dark, brooding look on its clean-shaven face and not the trace of a smile. Out of principle, presumably, because a smile is merely another ornament." That is right. These words show how different our views of beauty are. For me Beethoven's clean-shaven face with not the trace of a smile is more beautiful than all the laughing cavaliers of the Künstlerhaus[4] with their Vandykes. Solemn and serious the buildings of Vienna should look, as they have always looked solemn and serious. Enough of these fancy-dress balls, enough of this tomfoolery. I want to do away with frivolity in architecture.

And that brings me back to the clean-shaven face. Herr Epstein had submitted the smooth façade and it had been approved.

At the same time, to show how the façade might be decorated, we had submitted one with a horizontal wave pattern, a so-called "running dog." When the roof had been completed, and aroused great indignation among the citizens of Vienna, who could not understand why there were no cupolas, one of the gentlemen in the building control department seems to have lost his nerve and, when the wave pattern did not appear on the top story, took out an injunction in August 1910, stopping further work on the building.

I would just like to point out that what for centuries was accepted as the purpose of submitting plans and having them approved has been misunderstood by the authorities in recent years. The façade had to be submitted to stop vulgar show-offs, and there have always been some among architects' clients, from flaunting their bad taste, just as the sumptuary laws only came into being in order to curb ostentation. The clothes and houses that were permitted to the nobility were forbidden to commoners. Simple dress and simple houses were everyone's prerogative. No one felt compelled to be extravagant. And it is to this wise decree that the old towns owe their beauty. Beside the palaces of the aristocracy are the simple, plain houses of the ordinary citizens, setting off the beauty of the palaces. One spoke, the rest were silent. Now everyone is shouting his head off and no one can be heard.

If a commoner had submitted towers and cupolas, they would not have been allowed. Today, however, building control takes the opposite view of its function. In vain we pointed to the plain façade that the department had approved. Having no desire to take the matter to court, we resubmitted the original façade, though with somewhat lower windows since the original mezzanine floor had been raised at the insistence of the authorities, because it was subdivided. Then we had added roller shutters, making the windows five centimeters lower. But now this elevation was not approved. There had in the meantime been vehement criticism of the almost square windows, and newspapers in all seriousness flattered me with the invention of the three-light window. One writer found the "quadrangular windows" outrageous, which surprised people outside Vienna since until now houses with triangular windows have only been built in Hicksburg.

Windows with three lights are always nearly square and until now no one has ever seen this as a blemish. I blame the decorative style of the so-called modern Viennese movement which has so abused the square that it has brought this splendid shape into disrepute. That I, the main opponent of this mistaken, uncultured trend, should be the one to suffer is unpleasant. Since the square has lost its effectiveness they have thrown it on the scrap heap and are now turning their attention to degrading other shapes. I refuse to be put off by all this. Their main interest is, or was, in the square, that is as something to play around with. I make windows and divide up the panes. If that produces something like a square, then that was not the intention I set out with. Just as a plant grows the way it does, whether it wants to or not.

But something unexpected happened in city hall. The whole matter had been taken out of the hands of building control and given to the city council. The old façade was rejected on the pretext that the windows were now five centimeters lower. The city council turned to Herr Schneider, a specialist in building matters who was a member of the council, and asked him to tell them what they wanted. His answer was a vertical articulation. Asked what he thought it should look like, Councilman Schneider drew a façade over the empty façade.

Goldman and Salatsch had to lodge a deposit of 40,000 crowns for the completion certificate. It was stipulated that, taking the winter into account, the façade had to be completed by the following July, failing which the city would use the deposit to carry out the work itself.

The marble finally arrived during the winter. I had chosen it myself from the ancient quarries in Euboea, which were rediscovered by the English only ten years ago. There was worldwide delight at this discovery. People had been searching the world over for this most magnificent stone, used for ancient columns, and I thought the Viennese would be pleased to see some here. But not having seen this kind of stone before, they assumed it was synthetic. At a meeting of the city council one of the councilmen asked the burghermaster how he could countenance such an abomination of a building? The councilman was called Ryckl, so I immediately looked him up in Lehmann,[5] since I wanted to demonstrate the quality of the marble to him personally. There I read, "Ryckl, Karl, sculptor and producer of synthetic stone." I immediately abandoned the idea.

In the spring I went to Africa, to see the ancient Numidian onyx quarries, which had recently been rediscovered. During this absence my clients, seeing the day come ever closer when the city would spend their 40,000 crowns sticking on Herr Schneider's façade, announced a competition to get elevations for the façade.

The Association of Austrian Architects sent out an appeal calling on all reputable architects not to participate. There being no reason why my clients should have the façade of a disreputable architect stuck on their building, the panel of judges resigned. At that point the art critic of *Der Morgen* wrote, "Now Loos has all right-thinking people on his side." He was wrong, but July 1 came and the building control department did nothing.

As I said earlier, my clients had been given a completion certificate in return for a deposit. In the course of the winter completion was confirmed story by story, room by room. When, however, in the middle of July the clients sought the completion certificate for their own business premises, it was not granted, the reason given being that the façade was not completed. Legal proceedings would have taken months. In order to be able to move in they had to lodge a further 40,000 crowns deposit. This money was to be forfeited if the Schneider façade, or another, had not been begun before August 15.

Councilman Schneider's façade was impossible. With a few casual strokes of the pencil he took the carefully thought through architecture of the lower part of the building to absurd extremes. The main axes, which I had masked by placing such a strong emphasis on a large expanse of wall, were now to be made plain to everyone. I therefore suggested bronze window boxes, though not for all the windows. These window boxes are an Austrian feature, you see them very often in the country and in small towns. They were to be bronze, echoing the material of the roof, and of the coats of arms, light fittings, capitals and bases of the central section. But Councilman Schneider reported on the two proposals and decided in favor of his own. And that was the one the council approved.

I'm a strong man, I could take it. But my stomach couldn't. And I don't mean that figuratively. By the end of July my stomach was already rejecting its food. It was my stomach nerves. Eventually there was heavy bleeding and I was losing blood by the liter. I expected to die, but then the unexpected happened.

The deputy burghermaster, who was acting burghermaster during the summer, had heard of my condition. He called a meeting of the council at the last moment, on August 15, and got them to agree to postpone the whole matter until May 1. He saved my life. The deputy burghermaster was Dr Purzer.

My health has long since recovered. I have often wondered whether Councilman Schneider really is the man qualified to pass judgment on my façade. True, he did win the competition for the façade of the Technical Museum and is carrying it out. As it is a well-known fact that I know nothing about architecture, I asked two German architects to give me their opinion of the façade (since that is what is at issue in my case) of the Technical Museum. The two I asked were the most distinguished architect in Berlin, Ludwig Hoffmann, director of the city building department, and the most distinguished in Dresden, Professor Martin Dülfer, Wallot's[6] successor.

Ludwig Hoffmann writes,

"Berlin, December 4, 1911

I would very much regret it if such a building were to be erected opposite the palace of Schönbrunn.

It would not only result in a very unsightly building, it would also very much spoil the effect of the beautiful palace of Schönbrunn.

Ludwig Hoffmann."

Professor Dülfer writes:

"Dresden, November 27, 1911

It is proof of our low opinion of art that such a project can even be discussed seriously.

Martin Dülfer."

The judgment of Professor Gabriel von Seidel[7] is not available, as he is away. I will pass it on to the press later.

When I read these responses I cheered up and quickly got well again.

The battle of the building caused a great stir. Some people in Vienna poured scorn on it, but most waited for it to be finished before coming to a judgment. There were hardly any comments of an offensive nature. Criticisms such as that by a lady who wrote, at a time when none of the pillars were yet in place, "Certainly the building has been completely botched (as two prominent architectural experts told me)" did not hurt because everyone could identify the two architectural experts. Had they known they would appear in brackets as the pronouncers of this judgment they would have spared themselves the interview with the lady and the libel action. She tried to make good her error in a later essay, in which she wrote that no one should show a fool an uncompleted building.

But there was one piece of offensiveness which I feel I must put on record. It was not, however, a journalist, but an outsider who wrote:

... *in contrast to the logical structure of the imperial residence, where the crucial elements of the architectural concept, the pillars and beams, are never so aggressively displayed as to destroy the pleasant proportions of a façade, the building on Michaelerplatz, which has attained local notoriety, is an example of the use of a pseudo-structure to hide the real structure behind a decorative front. The problem is that the quite natural endeavor to make an externally visible dividing line between the lower shop windows and the upper, residential part of the house has been done in a very amateur fashion. What should always be avoided is here all too visible: the crude, unarticulated mass of the upper building seems to be trying to crush the marble and bronze splendor of the lower portion, especially since the brightly colored panels fitted over the ground floor premises, like any colored cladding plates, further reduce the feeling of a supporting structure ...*

To the vituperative tone of the media campaign against the architect, Adolf Loos, one is tempted to say with Tertullian when he attacked heretical doctrines, "One should treat such opposing views with mockery, for to treat them seriously would make them look important. Nothing deserves mockery more than pride" ...

The vituperative media campaign exists in the mind of the author of these lines alone. All of the 600 newspapers from home and abroad have taken my side, some even praising it effusively.

Only three have come out against it: the *Neue Freie Presse,* the *Extrablatt* and *Kikeriki.* And only a few months previously this man had congratulated me and proposed showing the house to architects as a model to be copied.

What caused him to use the *Neue Freie Presse* for a petty private feud is something I do not propose to discuss here.

In what style is the building? The Viennese style of 1910. People don't know that. They look for bizarre models in far-off countries, just as they looked for American models for my Café Museum. But in both cases I collected features from old Viennese coffee houses and façades in order to find the modern, the truly modern style. A hundred years ago it was tailors and architects who had it. Today it is only the tailors. But buildings have changed just as much as coats have. No more, no less. That is, very little. And if the Viennese would only look properly they would see that there is no great difference between the style of this building and the style of St. Michael's.

The wall at the back is not by me but by Hetzendorf von Hohenberg, the last great Viennese architect, and I want to pick up where he left off. It is true that the building has a different function from buildings in the past. That is expressed in it, just as the earlier function was expressed in earlier buildings. The main emphasis today is on the ground floor. That is where the architecture must make its strongest statement. Everything above is secondary. Nowadays no one has the time to look at statues and figures on the roof. The drivers of automobiles are against them as well. I know that forty years ago, when the Viennese were more appreciative of monumentality and the Ringstraße was built in accordance with that, there would have been no such storm of indignation. If, on the other hand, the Ring had been built ten years ago we would not have a Ringstraße but an architectural disaster. It signifies Vienna, the imperial city, the great metropolis. But the Stubenring is just Mährisch-Ostrau raised to six stories.

The most important authoritative verdict seems to me to be the one in the annual report of the Central Commission for

Artistic and Historical Monuments.

The popular name for it is "the house with no eyebrows." But don't take this mockery to heart, you dear old Viennese buildings with no eyebrows. Popular opinion has discovered that all you old buildings, you buildings on Franziskanerplatz, are flawed. But there are people who take the opposite view to popular opinion, people who think Franziskanerplatz is a little gem.

Some people also hold it against me that I have taken no account of Palais Heberstein.[8] Although the imperial palace does not need to be considered in relation to my building, since the two cannot be seen at the same time, I would at least like to point out that a simple structure does more for Fischer von Erlach's cupolas than another cupola would.

I would like to thank all those who have stood by me through this difficult time. To one man I owe a particular debt of thanks, a man remarkable for his generosity of spirit and modern outlook, who spoke out and wrote in support of the building at every opportunity, a man who represents good old-fashioned Viennese common sense, Herr Bielohlawek, a member of the Lower Austrian cabinet. Until now common sense has always come out on top. Recently two men were standing outside the building, one of whom was clearly very much worked up about it.

The Other: But it's a beautiful building.

The Opponent (vehemently): Well, yes, now. But you should have seen it earlier! You should have seen the façade that architect fellow stuck on. The city council made him scrape it all off. Now of course it looks all right.

The Other: So that's the way it was.

That's the way it was with all the buildings the Viennese are proud of today. That's the way it was with the Opera. One of its architects was made ill by the unending attacks and finished up in a lunatic asylum, the other committed suicide.[9] I am made of sterner stuff. I am not afraid for myself. I am afraid for the architects a hundred years from now. Which of them will be beaten to death with my Michaelerplatz building in a hundred years time?

Notes

1. The Michaelerkirche on the opposite side of Michaelerplatz.

2. Originally a summer residence of the Liechtenstein family, designed by Martinelli around 1700 (see also "The Discovery of Vienna"), just outside the city center in the 9th district, the Alsergrund.

3. Presumably the reference is to Joseph August Lux, 1871-1947, a journalist who wrote on a variety of cultural topics, especially art, and author of rather high-flown novels on the lives of famous writers and musicians.

4. The main art institute in Vienna, from which the members of the *Sezession* seceded in 1897.

5. Adolf Lehmann, 1828-1904, a journalist who published the first general directory of Vienna, which became known by his name.

6. Paul Wallot, 1841-1912; his most famous building was the Berlin *Reichstag*.

7. 1848-1913, active in Munich and Bavaria, where he designed many important buildings, including the Bavarian National Museum.

8. On Michaelerplatz between Herrengasse and Schäuflergasse, the building between Loos's and the *Hofburg*. Rebuilt in the mid-1890s, it housed the famous Café Griensteidl, the meeting place of the writers known as *Jung-Wien*, the most famous of whom were Schnitzler and Hofmannsthal.

9. Siccardsburg went mad and van der Null committed suicide.

18. The Mystery of Acoustics (1912)

I was asked whether the Bösendorfer Saal should be preserved. I presume what prompted the question was the idea that reverence for the past demands we should not demolish a hall that has played such an important role in the musical history of Vienna.

But it is not a question of reverence for the past, it is a question of acoustics. And that is the question I propose to answer. It was a good thing I was asked, otherwise I would have taken the answer to the grave with me.

For centuries architects have been working on the problem of acoustics. They tried to solve it on the drawing board. They drew straight lines from the sound source to the ceiling, assuming the sound would bounce off at the same angle, like a billiard ball from the cushion, and continue on its way. But all these diagrammatic representations are nonsense.

The acoustics of a hall do not depend on the spatial design, but on the material. A hall with poor acoustics can be improved by soft fabrics, by curtains and wall-coverings. Even a piece of thread strung across the middle of a hall can completely change the acoustics of the space and improve them.

But these are only makeshift solutions. The soft fabrics absorb the sound, taking away its fullness. The Greeks knew better. At regular intervals under the seats in their theaters they had sound-chambers containing huge metal bowls covered with drum skins. They tried to amplify the sound, not diminish it. And the Bösendorfer Saal has the most magnificent acoustics without any curtains at all, just straight, bare walls.

Perhaps what should be done, then, is to build a new hall using the exact measurements of the old one — to satisfy the supporters of the previous theory of acoustics — and using the same materials — to satisfy me. Certain result: a hall with terrible acoustics.

This kind of thing has already been tried. In Manchester they made an exact copy of the Bremen concert hall, which is world-famous for having the best acoustics. With negative results. But until now *every* new hall has had poor acoustics. Many of you will remember the opening of the Opera in Vienna. People complained that the house had such poor acoustics it would mean the end of the singer's art in Vienna. And today it is considered a model theater for acoustics.

Have our ears changed? No, it is the material the hall is made from that has changed. For forty years the material has absorbed good music and has been impregnated with the sound of the Philharmonic and the voices of our singers. These are mysterious changes in molecular structure which until now have only been observed in the wood violins are made of.

Does that mean that to give a space good acoustics you have to play music in it? No, that is not enough. You have to play *good* music in it. You can fool people, but you can't fool materials. Halls in which only brass bands have played will always have poor acoustics. And materials are very sensitive. You only have to let a military band blast away in the Bösendorfer Saal for a week and its celebrated acoustics will have gone to pot. Just as a ham-fisted amateur would ruin a violin that had belonged to Paganini. As a matter of general principle brass music is bad for building materials. That is why one side of opera houses is always poorer acoustically. With time halls in which brass instruments never play develop the best acoustics. The tones of Liszt and Messchaert live on in the mortar of the Bösendorfer Saal and vibrate with every note of a new pianist or singer.

That is the mystery of the hall's acoustics.

19. *Heimatkunst* (1912)

Architects have come to a dead end with their reproductions of old styles and now, after vainly having tried to discover the style of our times, they have come to another dead end. In this situation the catchword *Heimatkunst* — our own vernacular art — appears to offer them one last way out. I hope that will be the end of it. I hope that means the devil's arsenal is finally exhausted. I hope they will finally look to their own selves.

Heimat — home, where we belong — is a fine-sounding word and the demand that we foster our own, vernacular way of building quite justified. No foreign body should dare to force its way into a townscape, no Indian pagoda flaunt itself out in the countryside. But how do the artists who call themselves *Heimat-künstler* interpret this approach to art? First and foremost by banishing all technical progress from building for all time. New inventions, new experiences are not to be exploited because . . . well, because they are not part of vernacular art. It is fortunate for these architects that Stone-Age man did not insist on that, since it would mean there would be no vernacular architecture and they would not be able to make a living from it.

The Häusler-type roof cladding,[1] an epoch-making advance which, if it had come in the seventeenth century would have been greeted with jubilation by all architects, is rejected by our *Heimatkünstler*. After all, none of the other architects have any idea what to do with it either. Three hundred years ago, when the Italian style crossed the Alps, our Viennese architects and builders groaned at the problems the shingle roof posed to their powers of invention. In order to combat the northern snow and rain they tried tiles set in mortar, they raised false walls over the gable ends and inserted false windows. For centuries they longed for the flat roof. However by the time a simple merchant from Hirschberg in Silesia, following the great fire in Hamburg,[2] had solved the problem of the cheap, fireproof and waterproof flat roof, this centuries-old longing had disappeared. Truly, when the great moment came, it found a race of pygmies. They had no use for a flat roof. That is not necessarily a disaster. But what is a

disaster for civilization is that there are legislators in Germany
who have given way to pressure from the folksy *Heimatkünstler*
and banned the Häusler roof-cladding. For aesthetic reasons. Out
in the country tiles or slates are *de rigueur*.

In Vienna architects are ruining the city of their own free
will, without being compelled to do so by the authorities. They
are taking all the grandeur from the city. If I stand outside the
Opera and look down Schwarzenbergplatz I am filled with the
feeling, "This is Vienna! Vienna, the great metropolis, Vienna,
the capital of a great empire." But when I turn my head and look
at the apartment houses on Stubenring all I feel is: "Mährisch-
Ostrau raised to six stories."

And this is my first complaint against our *Heimatkünstler*:
they want to reduce our cities to small towns, small towns to
villages. But we should be moving in the opposite direction, just
as a barber's assistant, when choosing his clothes, is guided by the
desire to be taken for a count, while no count would choose his
clothes in order to be taken for a barber's assistant. This simple
principle, this desire for elegance, and therefore perfection, that
has motivated mankind from earliest times, has brought us to our
present level of culture. But the *Heimatkünstler* goes in the
opposite direction. The same details, the same roof-shapes, oriels,
towers and gables that have been used out in Mährisch-Ostrau
since there have been four-story houses, are now employed in the
capital.

The old Ringstraße is not exactly an architectural masterpiece. Stone forms are cast in cement and pinned on, an error it
shares with recent Viennese buildings. But the buildings of the
1870s were modeled on the palaces of the Italian aristocracy, just
as the buildings of the eighteenth century were. That gave us a
Viennese style, a style for a capital city. My building on Michaelerplatz may be good or bad, but there is one thing even its
opponents must allow: it is not provincial, it is a building that
could only be in a great metropolis. My country, right or wrong.
Right or wrong — my city.

However our architects show no longing for the Viennese

architectural style. They all subscribe to German architectural journals and the results are horrifying. Recently buildings have appeared in the city centre which have been imported straight from Magdeburg or Essen in the Ruhrgebiet. If the good people of Magdeburg are willing to put up with such buildings, then that is their affair, but here in Vienna we surely have the right to protest against them.

These buildings all have one thing in common: the articulation is vertical. The Germans have all been hypnotized by the Wertheim department store. Such a style may be appropriate in Berlin, the city with the endlessly long streets; the vertical articulation cuts up the long frontages and provides welcome points of rest for the eye. But in Vienna, the city of short streets (I am only talking of the central district), the eye demands a horizontal articulation of the façades. As Robert Örley has quite rightly pointed out, the Graben has been ruined for ever by the new building on the corner with Habsburgergasse. The baroque Column of the Holy Trinity stands on the Graben and it is quite obvious that such a column demands a horizontal background. But they put up a building which, when you are coming from Stephansplatz, provides the least favorable background imaginable. Coming from the Kohlmarkt you see another genuine German import in place of the old Trattnerhof.

I am for the traditional manner of construction. A model building for the Graben is the Savings Bank.[3] After it had been built the tradition was abandoned. That is where we should pick it up again. Have there been changes? There certainly have! They are the same changes as the ones that have created our new culture. No man can repeat a work. Each new day creates man anew and the new man is incapable of making the same thing as the old man created. He believes he is making the same thing and it turns into something new. Something imperceptibly new, but after a hundred years the difference can be perceived.

Are there no conscious changes?

Yes, there are. My pupils know that a change from the traditional way of doing things is only permissible if the change is an improvement. And the improvements, the new inventions are tearing huge holes in the tradition, in the traditional way of building. The new inventions — the electric light, the Häusler-type roof— do not belong to one particular region, they belong to the whole world.

So therefore the new intellectual and artistic trends also belong to all the inhabitants of the world. The sham of *Heimatkunst,* of a local, vernacular art, was foreign to the architects of the Renaissance. They all built in the Roman style. In Spain and Germany, in England and Russia. And in so doing they created the style of their own countries with which the people of today want to stifle any further development.

Genuine vernacular art is not even harmed by foreign artists working in the country. Even though they were all built by Italian architects and craftsmen, the Belvedere and the Renaissance hall of the Palais Waldstein in Prague are quite rightly counted as belonging to the German Renaissance and the Palais Liechtenstein behind the Burgtheater is the most beautiful and most monumental example of Viennese Baroque. There is a mysterious process at work here which until now has been ignored by psychologists and therefore remains unexplained. As we can see, even in a foreign city a craftsman should simply follow his own conscience, the rest he can happily leave to the air he breathes.

How should an architect from the metropolis build if he is asked to design a building out in the country? "Like a peasant," the *Heimatkünstler* says.

Let us look at the way a peasant goes to work. He marks out the plot where the building is to stand and digs out the foundations. The bricklayer puts one stone on another and in the meantime the carpenter sets up his workshop there. He makes the roof. A beautiful roof? An ugly roof? He has no idea. A roof, that's all.

Then the joiner comes and measures up the windows and doors, and all the other workmen come and measure up and go to their workshops and work. And when everything is in place, the peasant takes his brush and paints his house nice and white.

But the architect cannot work like that. He works according to a set design. And if he tried to copy the naïveté of the peasant he would get on everyone's nerves, just as much as the fine ladies in *dirndls* parading along the streets of Bad Ischl or stockbrokers jabbering away in Upper Austrian dialect.

This faux naïveté, this deliberate lowering of standards to an earlier cultural stage, is undignified and ridiculous and was therefore foreign to the old craftsmen, who were never undignified and ridiculous. Just take a look at the old manor houses and country churches built by town architects. They were always built in the same style the architect used in the town. Think of the Weilburg in Baden, of the churches built at the beginning of the 19th century in Lower Austria. How splendidly they blend into the landscape, while the childish attempts of the architects of the last forty years to truckle to nature with steep roofs, oriel windows and other yokelish yodelings have failed miserably. Even the Temple to the Hussars[4] fits in with the character of the Vienna Woods while every lookout tower in the style of a ruined castle defiles the hill it stands on. The Temple to the Hussars is truth, an imitation of a ruined castle a lie, and nature only tolerates truth.

However, instead of carrying our latest cultural and intellectual achievements, our new inventions and experience out into the country, the *Heimatkünstler* is trying to import the rural style of building into the city. He and his kind find rustic houses exotic, what they refer to with the word *picturesque*. But it is only to us that the country dwellers' clothing, furnishings and houses appear picturesque. The people who live in the country do not find themselves or their houses picturesque. They never built in a picturesque style, but now the city architects do nothing else. Picturesque are the irregular windows, the rough, weather-beaten walls, the old roof tiles. And all this is imitated in the city, according to the dictates of *Heimatkunst*. The regulations allow six stories, but we, in rural mode, create the illusion that the building has fewer and only make five. The sixth floor? That is under the roof, covered by roof tiles, and all the tricks of the trade are used to give them the wear and tear of a hundred years. And the genuine *Heimatkünstler* will also make sure it has proper green moss. And not forget the obligatory houseleek on the roof to protect it from lightning. I can already see the time coming when our office blocks and apartment houses, our theaters and concert halls will all be roofed with shingles and straw. *Rus in urbe* — it's a disgrace.

It is horrifying, the things that appear in our city and its suburbs under the slogan of vernacular architecture. The elegant style in which our greatgrandparents' generation built their houses in Hietzing and Döbling has been forgotten and a riot of Rococo scrollwork, balconies, amusing ideas for corners, oriel windows, gables, turrets, roofs and weathervanes has been unleashed on the unsuspecting landscape. One subscribes to an American journal and builds with ashlar which, however, does not come from the Rocky Mountains but has been neatly carved and chiseled at Soandso's (Stonemasons to the Imperial Court) until it looks just like the Wild West. Another takes the *Studio* and builds so-called "bird houses," see-through houses which even from a distance reveal their ground plan and its most private rooms to the observer's eye. And they would all prefer to thatch their roofs, you can't get more *Heimat* than that. *Le dernier cri.*

In a few days one of the last Hietzing houses will be torn down. It is adjacent to the Schönbrunn Park Hotel and the site is needed for an extension. What culture that house embodied, what refinement! How Viennese, how Austrian, how human! And therefore how "Hietzingish!" The authorities frown on people sticking to tradition. It is well known that such buildings have no façade and they don't like that. They like people imitating all the other parvenus, they want each to drown out the other.

Only this summer the plans for a dwelling house in Hietzing were rejected by the Commission with the following words: "The building lacks the picturesque façade usual in this area through the addition of roofs, turrets, gables and oriel windows. For this reason planning permission is withheld."

Higher authority, however, takes a different view, and Viennese architects cannot use the Department of Building to justify their ruining the suburbs.

This new obsession with working in the style of Berlin-Grunewald or Munich-Dachau I call Munichery-knackery — Viennese it certainly is not. So much Italian air has blown over the Alps to us that we should build like our fathers in a style that shuts the house off from the outside world. Not only Italian buildings do that (apart from the Venetian ones), but also all the German ones. Only French houses, which our architects always have in mind as models, cannot do too much to reveal their ground plans.

A roof in Austria should have a low pitch. People in the Alps have the shallowest pitch in order to deal with the wind and snow. As a matter of course, therefore, our *Heimatkünstler* put the steepest possible roofs on them, roofs that are a positive danger to those living under them every time it snows. Shallow roofs enhance the beauty of our mountain regions, steep roofs impair it. A remarkable example of how what is intrinsically right leads to what is aesthetically right.

There remains something to be said about materials. I was criticized by one of the highest of the higher-ups for the fact that, despite the emphasis I put on the vernacular side of my Michaelerplatz building, I had brought marble from Greece. But Viennese cuisine is Viennese even though it uses spices from the Far East, and a building can be genuine, that is, Viennese, even if its copper roof comes from America. But this objection cannot be so easily brushed aside. It would be wrong to use red brick for a building in Vienna. Not because we do not have brick, we do, but because we have something better, namely plaster rendering. In Danzig, despite its tradition of brick building, plaster rendering would be permissible; in Vienna I would be wrong to leave the walls unrendered. I can take my materials from anywhere, at any point I can exchange a technique for a better one.

Instead of following spurious catchwords such as *"Heimatkunst,"* we should finally make up our minds to follow the one truth I keep on proclaiming: tradition. We should condition ourselves to build as our fathers built and not be afraid of being old-fashioned. We are more advanced than the peasant. It is not only our threshing machines he needs, he should also share in our knowledge and our experience in building. We should be leading him on, not aping him.

It is time all this spurious activity — which reaches its nadir in amateur folk theatricals with their brightly colored peasant fabrics, designed after candy wrappings, with their sham naïveté, their contrived stammering instead of speaking freely, with their childish masquerades, which can be seen in the fact that those who run our School of Applied Art are rightly celebrated as the supreme authority on rocks made from papier mâché and grass from strips of canvas — it is time all this childish babble that goes under the name of *Heimatkunst* stopped.

We work as well as we can without pausing for a moment to think about the form. The best form is always there already and no one should be afraid of using it, even if the basic idea for it comes from someone else. Enough of our geniuses and their originality. Let us keep on repeating ourselves. Let one building be like another. We won't be published in *Deutsche Kunst und Dekoration* and we won't be made professor of applied art, but we will have served ourselves, our times, our nation and mankind to the best of our ability. And that means we will have served our *Heimat* too.

Notes

1. A type of roofing using layers of paper, sand and gravel stuck together with *Holzzement* (60% coal-tar, 25% sulphur, 15% asphalt).
2. In 1842.

3. Presumably the Post Office Savings Bank, built by Otto
Wagner in 1904-06; it is not on the Graben but in the Stuben
Quarter of the central district. Loos is citing it as the type of
building suitable for the Graben.

4. The first war memorial to the unknown soldier in Austria,
erected in 1813 to the hussars who fell in the Napoleonic Wars.
Designed by Josef Kornhäusel, it is in the style of a Doric temple
and stands on the edge of the Vienna Woods between Hinter-
brühl and Mödling.

20. My School of Building (1913)

There is no greater misfortune than to be condemned to inactivity.

When, fifteen years ago, I asked Professor Josef Hoffmann to be allowed to do the interior design for the *Sezession* committee room, which no one sees and on which only a few hundred crowns were going to be spent, my request was turned down flat.

When, through the good offices of Wilhelm Exner,[1] I was given the opportunity of lecturing to the participants in the tailoring course at the Technological Museum, the then secretary, Dr. Adolf Vetter (now in the Labor Department), insisted I stop immediately.

This second experience was the more painful. I felt I had something to offer my fellow men, not just through my example, but in my teaching as well. And this pain turned into torment when I saw how examples of my work, which gradually came to the public eye through a number of commissions, were twisted into a false doctrine.

A ray of light! Some of Otto Wagner's pupils, in my opinion the best, suggested I apply for the chair he had vacated.

Naturally I was well aware the attempt was doomed to failure, but the confidence the flower of our younger generation showed in me gave me the strength to set up my own school.

That is how the Adolf Loos School of Building came into being.

I want to replace the method taught at our academies, which consists partly of the adaptation of past architectural styles to modern requirements and partly of a search for a new style, with my own teaching: tradition.

At the beginning of the nineteenth century we departed from tradition. That is where I want to go back to.

Our culture is founded on the recognition of the all-transcending greatness of classical antiquity. Our manner of thinking and feeling we have adopted from the Romans, who taught us to think socially and discipline our emotions.

Since mankind has come to recognize the greatness of classical antiquity, the great architects have all had the same approach. "The way I build," they thought, "is the way the Romans would have gone about it in my situation." This is the approach I want to instill in my students.

The present should build on the past, just as the past built on previous generations.

It was never otherwise, nor will it ever be. It is truth that I am teaching. Because of the false doctrines which have taken over all schools and the public, I will not live to see the victory of truth. Whether my students will, depends on their strength. I warn all those who lack this strength against becoming my students. They will have to make their own way, excluded from the cliques which, with their clubs, associations, art journals and the newspapers, have conquered the public. They will be excluded from state commissions and professorships. I only hope the feeling of having dedicated their lives to society's most pressing needs will be full compensation for titles, honors and sinecures.

I have regular students, who work in my office, and auditors, who can attend my lectures. I derive great satisfaction from the fact that the students of our two state schools of architecture, the Technical University and the Academy, are well represented in my audience. Three subjects have been taught so far: interior work, art history and materials. The Schwarzwald Schools put their classrooms at my disposal, for which I would like to express my heartfelt thanks, and those of my students, to the director, Dr. Eugenie Schwarzwald. The school must have had a great deal to put up with. There was such a crowd that my lectures had to be held in two rooms, joined by double doors, each holding forty people. But it was a big success. My audience came from all social classes; visitors from abroad who were in Vienna for a short time wanted to hear me; poor students sat next to princesses.

In the middle of the academic year one of the teachers at our Technical University forbade his students to attend my lectures. I owe him a debt of thanks. Those with minds of their own stayed and he rid me of the rest.

I only had three full-time students. One had completed the Higher Trade School, two had done a few semesters at the Technical University, but had no technical knowledge of building. My method of approaching a project is to go through all the technical and architectural details at once. The design of the exterior goes back to the point where Viennese architects departed from tradition. Herr von Wagner deliberately chose the Doric style, Herr Engelmann[2] the Ionic. It is part of the ethos of the school that students compare their work, that they learn from each other. Their projects had to be designed from inside outwards, floors and ceiling (parquet and coffering) were the primary elements, the façade secondary. Great weight was laid on the smallness of the axes (in the ceiling and windows) and on the right furnishings. In this way I taught my students to think three-dimensionally, in the cube. Few architects today can do that; thinking in surfaces seems to be the be-all and end-all of an architect's education.

Next year I intend to expand my school of building. Structural mechanics and the principles of building construction will also be taught so that students can come straight from the high schools and technical high schools. Finally, in each year a Viennese building will be looked at as a whole, a building from the period to which we should go back to pick up the tradition. Next year the series will start with Hetzendorf von Hohenberg's principal work, the Palais Pallavicini on Josefsplatz, which will then appear as a publication of my School of Building.

Notes

1. 1840-1931, founder and director of the *Technologisches Gewerbemuseum* (Technological Museum of Craft)

2. Students of Loos's school of building: Helmut Camillo von Wagner-Freynsheim, 1889-1968, and Paul Engelmann, 1891-1965, who collaborated with Wittgenstein on the house he built.

21. Rules for Building in the Mountains (1913)

Do not build in a picturesque manner. Leave that kind of effect to the walls, the mountains and the sun. A person who dresses picturesquely is not picturesque, but a clown. Country folk do not dress picturesquely, but they are picturesque.

*

Build as well as you can. Not better. Do not get ideas above your station. And not worse. Do not deliberately descend to a lower level than the one on which birth and education has placed you. Even when you go to the mountains. Talk to the country folk in your own language. The Viennese lawyer speaking to the locals in roadmender's dialect must be eradicated.

*

Take note of the forms in which the country folk build. They are wisdom from our forefathers, essence made manifest. But seek the reason for the form. If technical advance has made it possible to improve the form, then the improvement is always to be used. The flail is replaced by the threshing machine.

*

The plains demand the vertical articulation of buildings, the mountains horizontal. The works of man should not compete with the works of God. The Habsburgwarte[1] disrupts the chain of the Vienna Woods, the Husarentempel fits in harmoniously.

*

Do not think about the roof, but about rain and snow. That is how the country folk think and why in the mountains they give their roofs the shallowest pitch their technical experience tells them is possible. In the mountains the snow should not slide off whenever it feels like it, but when the inhabitants want. For that reason they must be able to climb up on the roof without endangering their lives to get rid of the snow. And we should create the shallowest roof possible according to *our* technical experience.

*

Be true. Nature is always on the side of truth. She gets on well with iron bridges with railings, but Gothic arches with turrets and embrasures she rejects.

*

Do not be afraid to be criticized for being old-fashioned. Changes in the old way of building are permissible only when they are improvements. Otherwise stick to things as they always have been. For truth, even if it be hundreds of years old, has a closer connection with our inner being than the untruth marching along beside us.

Notes

1. An observation tower on the Hermannskogel built by Franz von Neumann in 1889 in the style of a fortified watchtower complete with battlements etc. For the Husaren-tempel see footnote to chapter "*Heimatkunst.*"

22. Adolf Loos on Viennese Buildings

(From the notes of a participant in the guided tours Loos organized in 1913/14.)

Herrengasse

When you look at the beautiful dome of the Spanish Riding School and the buildings around which fit in so well, you can understand why I made my building on Michaelerplatz the way it is and how wrong the Heberstein building is, with its castle look and its dome.

The original function of Herrengasse was as a connection from the Kahlenberg to the River Wien. Before the Opera was built you could see St. Charles's from Herrengasse through the arch leading to Josefsplatz.

No. 5 Herrengasse is a town house belonging to Count Wilczek, built in 1750. No. 7, the Palais Modena, built 1810; in the vestibule are massive Tuscan columns, because of the enormous span; Ionic columns could not be thickened in the same way. No. 9, Palais Clary, around 1690. An interesting feature the two cast-iron parapets on the windows; all the ornaments are of stone, only the ornamental band is in plaster; still in sound condition today! No. 11, the Statthalterei,[1] built by Sprenger in 1845. With this building the tradition was abandoned. No. 13, the Landhaus,[2] built in 1837; nothing to write home about, but good enough; we should be glad we have it; between 1837 (Landhaus) and 1845 (Statthalterei) things started to run wild. Much better than the Landhaus, though, is no. 15. This really served as a model for me when I was designing my building on Michaelerplatz. It is very beautiful, the combination of ground floor and mezzanine very elegant, the upper part very simple, the roof truss has a very shallow pitch. No. 17, the Austro-Hungarian Bank, is also refined. The influence of classical antiquity is strongest in the marvelous portal; the Erechtheum was being excavated about the time it was built and that explains the purity and nobility of the influence; the joinery on the doors is excellent.

The Academy of Fine Arts

Built by Hansen in the 70s, his first monumental building. The rear view from Getreidemarkt is more effective because the building is much higher there. The granite socle is the most magnificent thing that has been built in Vienna in the modern period. The way Hansen has created a relationship between the arches of the rear façade and the windows of the side by placing them under one cornice is very elegant. With its four corner pylons supporting it and no projecting structure in the middle, the effect is monumental. None of our "moderns" could manage anything like that. I never pass the side entrance in Makartgasse without a feeling of admiration.

The building also has the correct position in relationship to Ringstraße: if you look across to it, you are filled with surprise, with a sense of grandeur, monumentality. And Ringstraße is on a higher level. If it were the other way round the view would be overpowering. Such sights enrich the city. But the *Burgtheater* pushing its way out into Ringstraße or the wrongly sited Goethe monument arouse no such feelings.

Notes

1. Offices of the provincial government of Lower Austria.
2. Parliament of the province of Lower Austria.

23. Winter Sports Hotel on the Semmering[1]

(From the notes of a participant in a seminar organized by Loos at the Schwarzwald School 1913/14.)

A bathroom with direct light and a window that does not give onto the ventilation shaft, but looks out onto the street, is a fine thing, certainly: a small chamber between two rooms that has been divided in two and added to the rooms. Such rooms are quite justifiably expensive since the partitioning is an extravagance and the upkeep costs for a bathroom are higher than those for an ordinary hotel room.

For a hotel in the mountains loggias are the best solution. Balconies are not because some people suffer from vertigo and balconies jutting out make them feel uncomfortable; you have to take both the height of the stories and of the mountain on which the hotel is built into account.

Servants' rooms and anterooms do not need direct light. Their light comes from windows high up on the wall giving onto the corridor. But it is dangerous for a hotel not to give the servants' rooms a good situation, for servants can turn their employers against a hotel, often the valet is the real master. For that reason servants' quarters should be provided which give onto the street or the courtyard. A hotel should not arrange to have servants' rooms which *only* give onto the courtyard.

This creates a zone of small rooms; a loggia with a room and bathroom. These rooms can be put to various uses: anteroom, servant's room, boxroom. Too few of the latter are generally provided. People don't go to a hotel in the mountains for two or three days, as they do in Vienna, but for two or three months, and they bring many changes of clothing with them, then don't know where to put their luggage. So the suitcases and trunks stand along the corridor, which doesn't look nice and is awkward when people go to get their clothes. The boxrooms could be rented out. There should be connecting doors between the rooms so that several rooms can be let together as a suite.

Quiet is of the utmost importance and the surest way of

achieving it is by building two walls with an air space between instead of just one.

It makes no difference to the cost if you make two 7 cm walls instead of one of 15 cm, but the gap of 7 cm makes 21 cm in all.

The doors are double doors, of course, and if two apartments are taken together they are removed and put in the storeroom. There must be a storeroom on every floor, for extra pieces of furniture which might be requested for the rooms: a sofa-bed, an extra bed, wardrobe etc. These things cannot be taken up in the elevator, certainly not in the passenger elevators, and elevators for goods are a rarity. The men have to lug them up on their shoulders.

In hotels there are rooms, anterooms, bathrooms, WCs, an indoor swimming pool — an American facility the Germans still cannot get used to — servants' rooms, storerooms — one on each floor — and rooms necessary for the functioning of the hotel on each floor.

On each floor there is a supervisor for the chambermaids. When guests ring for service it is one of her subordinates who comes, so that one is often completely unaware of her existence, then the waiter responsible for room service, the servant who cleans shoes and clothes, the chambermaid, the waiter who brings the food. Bedrooms have to be provided for these people and rooms where they can go about their business: sculleries and pantries. In small hotels it is not usual to have a supervisor for the chambermaids on every floor, just a porter and a supervisor for two or three floors.

Notes

1. A vacation area on a pass sixty miles south of Vienna.

24. The Hotel on Friedrichstraße, Vienna

(From the notes by a participant in a seminar organized by Loos at the Schwarzwald School, 1913/1914.)

The hotel could face onto Karlsplatz, since when the Nasch-markt[1] in front of it is moved, it will be replaced by a large park. There is one oblique corner so that St Charles's can be seen a few steps sooner although, given the unfortunate concept of the Ringstraße,[2] these couple of minutes make little difference. The vestibule is modeled on American hotels. It is an extension of the street and not exactly elegant. You don't take your hat off when you go in, people are running to and fro, there are piles of luggage, and people come in from the street to stand around, since it is very pleasant there, cool in summer and heated in winter. There are flower stalls, tobacco stores, bookshops, ticket agencies there, just as in the southern States. It all looks like a station concourse, only there is also a place for the porter, his desk and the keys are there.

Since the vestibule is a continuation of the street and it would be too time-consuming for the hotel staff to remove casual outsiders, they have made it possible to keep them apart from the hotel guests by a winter garden which is separated from the vestibule by being one floor lower but shares the same ceiling and overhead lighting. A corridor with the cloakrooms leads from the

Hotel on Friedrichstraße, Vienna. Façade.

winter garden to the dining room, which is also in the basement. This has a glass wall, so that you can see in from the vestibule, but guests are less disturbed by the people there than by those in the street. At the end of the vestibule is a staircase leading, on the right, to the private rooms, on the left to the banquet hall, then there is a series of drawing rooms for ladies and gentlemen, the former strictly segregated as smoking is forbidden in them. There is a further Viennese restaurant, a small store with a lot of gold, a café, a teashop, an American bar, a garage in the base-ment, small shops on the mezzanine floor.

Light from above is avoided as far as possible, as it can make life a misery during continuous rainy spells; that is what it is like here in the Hotel Bristol, for a life with electric lighting and light from above is impossible in the long run. They have not bothered much with staircases. There are two staircases and two servants' stairs, but the main thing is the elevator, for the people are carried up and down.

Notes

1. The food market. Originally adjoining the west end of Karlsplatz, it was later moved to a site on the Wienzeile.
2. See no. 12, "Appeal to the Citizens of Vienna."

25. Architecture and the Café

(From the notes of a participant in a seminar organized by Adolf Loos at the Schwarzwald School, 1913/14)

The usual Viennese café. How should it look outside? The thing by which the owner sets most store, the sign, is the least important of all. We people of the 19th and 20th century live in a quite different way from earlier times. We live on the horizontal, not upward.

The person to achieve the greatest effects is one who does not consider himself an artist. In Vienna it is better to have your café furnished by a furniture store than by an architect. The tasteless Astoria is good because it brings in money for the owner as it is right for the class of people who go there. Really outstanding is the Café Bristol, with furnishings by Bamberger's. Apart from the entrance, that's poor. But the interior is excellent because it doesn't try to be modern.

In earlier times people wanted to do everything in the café: play, read. Today there has been specialization. Our café is already specialized compared to the country café, and the more advanced a city, the more specialization there is. In Berlin there is a Billiards Palace. Kerkau, the famous billiards player, was paid millions to carry out the project. On the first floor there is a normal Viennese café, on the second one like the C. C.[1] — that is, a nighttime café that is almost always empty during the day — and on the next floor there are sixty-four billiard tables. The effect they make is remarkable. You think there are thousands. The good billiard players no longer play in small cafés where you also go for your coffee. The care of a billiard table is a science necessary to protect it from damage and the effects of the climate. The players go where the tables are well looked after and not to a place where the only upkeep is an occasional brushing from the billiard marker. The dimensions of billiard tables vary. The French ones, which we use here, keep on getting smaller. The English ones are very large. An English billiard table that was here for a year, but then went back, cost 65,000 crowns.

Notes

1. The Café Central in Vienna, the most important writers' café.

26. The Opening of the Technical Museum (1918)

Next Monday there is a surprise in store for the citizens of Vienna. The Technical Museum is going to be opened.

The building was finished many years ago. It is at the Hietzing end of Mariahilfer Straße, opposite Schönbrunn Palace. Driving past, people wondered why the doors were always shut. Then they remembered there is a war on.

But no, that was not the reason. Despite the war they were working inside the building as if it were peacetime. The Viennese will be amazed next Monday to see what has been done. In the way it is arranged and set out, in its wealth of instructive information and displays to arouse our curiosity it recalls the exhibition of hygiene in Dresden, which is the highest praise one can give an exhibition.

The Viennese have long since passed judgment on the exterior. That the building is not parallel to the street, but askew, is terrible. Otherwise they like it. As we read this morning, ". . . forming a harmonious counterpart to the historical elegance of Schönbrunn Palace." I — the man who disfigured the city with his Michaelerplatz building, who therefore has no taste and is not competent to judge architectural questions — would not dream of expressing my own opinion. Instead I will quote the Berlin Director of Building, Ludwig Hoffmann. He wrote, "I would very much regret it if such a building were to be erected opposite Schönbrunn Palace. It would not only result in a very unsightly building, it would also very much spoil the effect of the beautiful palace." And Professor Martin Dülfer from Dresden wrote, "It is proof of our low opinion of art that such a project can even be discussed seriously."

For the ground plan a system of rooms leading off corridors has been chosen and that is all to the good. It avoids the effect of a display of curiosities which a system of open halls encourages — see Munich. That all the effects of Munich can be achieved without theatrics and in a more practical manner, even here and for the visitor who genuinely wants to learn, is demonstrated by the displays of old workshops. We can see a brewery as it must have operated in the days of Tacitus (the water was heated in wooden vats by throwing in red-hot stones), we can see an old mill, an old scythe smithy. And what gems the museum has in the history of machines! And transport! An Austrian automobile of 1875 does not look all that old-fashioned. And how the Viennese will throng to have a peek into the drawing-room car of the late empress.

But the most popular will be the mine, if only because it recalls the wonders of the fairground train ride. Everything can be seen, the confusing labyrinth of the galleries, miners at work, the clattering hammer drill and the pit dog.

27. Guidelines for a Regulatory Body for the Arts (1919) (Excerpt)

Training as Master Builder and Architect

Following the new regulations, the state may only train those to qualify as master builders and architects who have completed an apprenticeship as bricklayer, carpenter or stonemason. To be accepted for entry to the schools the candidates have to pass an intelligence test. As at the present trade schools, which should be developed, teaching can go hand in hand with practical experience. Building should be abolished as a subject at the higher state trade schools.

For students of building at the Technical University, the summer semester should be left free for practical activities.

Only such students may be accepted at the Academy who can demonstrate they have sufficient experience of building and the architect's office. Conditions for students at the Academy will be the same as those for painters and sculptors.

Training as Designer

This task should be reserved to the School of Arts and Crafts in Vienna. The School of Arts and Crafts and that school alone should train designers for the various industries. The other technical schools do not have this responsibility, but should restrict themselves to the technical aspects of the trade they teach.

Once a student has learned a trade in a technical works or one of the technical schools, he should be sent to the School of Arts and Crafts in Vienna. Even if in later life he is going to remain tied to the place where his factory is situated, it is only in the great city — where all the modern trends converge, where he will be imbued with modern taste, which alone makes industry competitive in the world market, and where he will constantly see examples of the correct use of his products — that he can lay the foundations for a fruitful working life. Designers should only be trained for one specific trade (material). People who can invent designs in two materials will produce nothing worthwhile. We can all only think in one material.

The School of Arts and Crafts should not train architects, painters or sculptors.

Training as Craftsman

1. In an apprenticeship.

The best craft workshops should be compelled to accept a certain percentage of apprentices, based on their size. Workshops which produce poor work should be forbidden to take on apprentices.

Apprentice workshops should be set up for master craftsmen who have distinguished themselves by the excellence of their work, especially in the production of luxury goods. Firms will be directed to provide work for these apprentice workshops. This is particularly important in the transitional period following the end of the war, in order to avert the impending decline of our luxury goods industry.

2. In technical schools.

The technical school should only teach the modern style. There should be special technical schools set up for copying craftwork from older times; these should restrict themselves to specific periods.

The schools should be strictly specialized. Thus the schools for wood carving, for example, should be divided into those that deal with modern problems and those that teach how to copy old furniture, and even these latter should be separated into different styles. Creating new designs in old styles should be absolutely forbidden. These schools must confine themselves to copying in the strictest sense.

The Organization of the Professions

Questions concerning professional matters are to be settled under the supervision of the regulatory body. Associations could be set up, along the lines of the lawyers' associations, to deal with matters such as fees, competitions and professional conduct for artists, musicians and writers. Elections would be organized along the same lines as for the Press Office for the Arts.

The Care of Ancient Monuments

The protection of artistic and cultural monuments

Individual works of art

The register should be completed as quickly as possible.

Apart from the obligation, contained in the draft legislation of 1912, to inform the authorities before exporting a work of art, private owners should have the following obligations:

1. To give the state the right of inspection.

2. The obligation to preserve the work.

3. The obligation to report works for inclusion in the register.

4. The obligation to provide access for the public to larger collections.

In order to regulate the private art trade, private sellers should be given space to display their goods, if necessary by granting them loans. Apart from pawnbroking and auctions, the Dorotheum could also provide facilities for those who want to sell their own works of art.

Conservation of the city

Drastic changes in the character of the city should only be allowed for practical reasons, never for aesthetic reasons. Aesthetic reasons are subject to change, and since so far we have always been wrong, we will be wrong for evermore, and by the time we realize our mistakes it is too late to rebuild cultural monuments that have been destroyed. The Department of Ancient Monuments is responsible for the preservation of all monuments. New buildings only fit into the city harmoniously when they are done in the style of their times, that is, neither in kitschy echoes of old styles, nor in the authentic *Werkbund*[1] style (quality workmanship!). Buildings done in the style of their own times are those which carry on the traditional way of building we had before the imitation of different styles came in, but with the deliberate exploitation of the latest inventions and experience.

Especially valuable districts, squares, streets and fortifications are also required to be included in the register. All changes and new buildings require the approval of the Department of Artistic and Cultural Monuments.

Protection of Natural Monuments

Of individual monuments

"Tree days" are to be held in schools and in the course of his or her life each child is required to plant at least one tree, which must be marked so that adults can go and see the results of their labors throughout their lives. This would create such deep respect for the beauty of trees that it would make all laws against their wanton destruction in town and country superfluous.

Of the landscape

Commemorative towers (beehives) on the tops of hills and mountains are forbidden.

Lookout towers may not be built in the style of ruins or of Gothic towers.

Advertising billboards in meadows and woods are to be forbidden.

Where waterfalls are affected by industrialization, arrangements are to be made for the works to be closed down from time to time, allowing the waterfall to assume its natural form. Industrial installations are to be so sited as not to spoil the natural landscape.

Bridges are to be purely functional structures, with no echoes of a past style.

Notes

1. An association of artists, craftsmen and manufacturers set up in Munich in 1907, based on the ideas of William Morris and the English Arts and Crafts movement. See Loos's article "Surplus to Requirements" in the volume *Ornament and Crime*.

28. Art and Architecture[1] (1920)

The effect of works of genius on their contemporaries is not one of beauty, but of terror. They are not destined for our generation. But ordinary people have the right to surround themselves with objects they find beautiful, for they have need of such objects. Of course, they can live without pictures and without music, but they cannot live without shoes, without chairs, without a bed and without a roof over their heads.

Art exists — the future.

Industry exists — the present.

But industrial art, applied art does not exist. It is industry that produces the objects we use and wear out. Food and drink, automobiles and houses should look beautiful to those who possess them.

But a work of art should not be worn out by use. It is eternal. It should not be put to practical use so as not to lose its value. It should have the time it needs to fulfill its mission. It should last until such time as, by continually being seen, it has imposed itself on mankind. It will never become ugly because it has never been beautiful.

After it has been used, a work of industrial art will be abandoned and mocked by posterity. A woman will find it impossible that she can have thought a particular hat beautiful ten years ago. Works of industrial art go out of fashion.

But a work of art never goes out of fashion. It waits for its hour to come. For people to have raised themselves to its level.

From that moment onward it will grip our souls with a profound and edifying emotion until the last human heart has ceased to beat.

There are people with antimodern tastes, dawdlers, the back-markers of humanity, people who do not want to belong to their age. They regret the passing of times when objects of everyday use were still works of art. They talk of applied art.

Some of them copy old forms. They are the least dangerous. They are mere fools, as inoffensive as an old lady in crinoline and ankle-length drawers taking a walk on the boulevards.

The dangerous ones are those who want to bring back old times by demanding modern art in objects of everyday use. They are criminals in the domain of the spirit. They block the way forward for artists. They are the ones who alienate humanity from art. They are the ones who are responsible for the demand that art should be beautiful. For a person who can put a pair of shoes and a picture on the same level can never appreciate the beauties of a picture.

Humanity is resisting these people who are behind our civilized times. We don't want anything to do with their works. We don't want to know about this mixture of spirit and materialism. But there is one nation which has managed to make this mixture of art and industry, of spirit and matter, of God and money, a nation which feels at ease with this mixture: the German nation.

Over there everything is a work of art. Not a copy of old things, not the lady in her crinoline, but a modern work of art. They sit down on art, they spit into a spittoon which is the latest creation of Zapfer, a creation reproduced in the review *German Art and Decoration*. And in 1918 there was an exhibition which bore the proud title of *Art in the Service of Commerce*.

There are some people in France who look to Germany and regret that the same state of affairs does not exist in their country. They complain that the French cannot produce works of this kind.

But it is France's own genius which has preserved her from such barbarism, from such a return to the past. France has managed to defend herself successfully against these traitors.

An object of everyday use serves the present, a work of art is destined for the future. The object of everyday use has to be able to lose its value so that it can give way to another.

The form of any object of everyday use lasts, that is, does not displease the eye or, in the general expression, does not go out of fashion as long as the object lasts. Every craftsman knows this.

Dressmakers modify their styles more quickly than cabinetmakers. If the cabinetmaker changed his forms as quickly as the dressmaker, if one could not keep the cabinetmaker's creations until they had reached the end of their useful life, if we had to remove them from our apartments for aesthetic reasons, the work and the materials would be lost. We could start burning the works of Plumet and Selmersheim now. Politeness stops me from naming the "artists" whose works will fuel our stoves in twenty years time.

The craftsman who produces works that last is by that very fact conservative.

Gradually humanity has managed to draw a clear demarcation line between spirit and matter. The struggle between the two tendencies ended during the nineteenth century. Until then artist and artisan were one. Works of art were used and worn out. For people of today that is barbaric.

One after another all branches of industry were withdrawn from the domain of art. And now it is the turn of architecture.

Architecture was an art, nowadays it is no more an art than tattooing or shoemaking. For works of architecture are made to be used and worn out, they are made to please contemporary society.

Is this sad news I bring my colleagues? Have I caused them pain? I am an architect myself and the struggle to reach this truth was painful. But I have finished struggling and today I am a happy man. I know I am a craftsman whose task is to serve mankind and the present. But by that very fact I know that art exists. I know about art. I know that it cannot be created on demand, that it exists within itself. I can follow the flight of the artist as he disappears, like a condor, into the unknown — and I can pray.

Notes

1. Original in French.

29. Rules for Social Housing Developments (1920)

Every social housing development starts with the garden. The garden is the primary feature, the house secondary.

Only people who feel the need to work in their gardens, as well as in their regular occupations, in order to produce food have the right to take up land from society for themselves. Therefore they should be allowed to live in the same place as their gardens in order to increase their harvest. For them, this is a necessity. People who do not produce food belong in an apartment house.

Personal enjoyment of a garden must consist solely of growing food. The enjoyment of a garden in the sense of aesthetic pleasure must be sought in public parks. These two ways of enjoying a garden are opposites: on the one hand pleasure in the harvest (destroying nature) and on the other pleasure in natural growth (preserving nature).

Not everyone is suited to gardening. Garden work is an antidote to the nerve-destroying division of labor which allocates the constructive and destructive processes to different people. Garden work is the essential destructive complement for every worker engaged in a constructive process. Without it he will waste away, both spiritually and physically.

The land should not become the property of the individual. That would lead to the opposite of what is intended. Instead of satisfying people's right to destructive labor it would encourage property speculation. The land belongs to the cooperative on which every housing development is based.

In order to avoid the exploitation of personal connections, the right to build a house is not granted by the cooperative but by a body external to the cooperative. Only people who have maintained their gardens properly for a number of years will be given permission to build a house. Neglect of the garden will result in exclusion from the cooperative.

The houses will not be built from public funds, but from the savings made through garden produce. Everyone who is allocated land must accept the obligation of helping to reduce the housing shortage by building a house. Without this obligation, two classes of workers would be created: those who have to spend the whole of their weekly wages on food and those who can save part by working in their garden. That would run counter to the social character of the development.

But to those who have shown, by keeping up their work, that they intend to continue looking after their gardens, the state should give the nucleus of a house which they can then transform into a complete house by buying the component parts week by week. I have worked out a system which demands no greater skill than the ability to hammer in a nail, something that ought to be within the powers of every gardener. When the inhabitants move out, of their own free will or compulsorily, the purchase costs are to be reimbursed, with a deduction for wear and tear.

30. The House with One Wall (1921)

Builders distinguish between two kinds of wall: load-bearing walls and party walls. Load-bearing walls support the ceiling joists.

Party walls separate the house from its neighbor.

Load-bearing walls are made as massive as is necessary to support the ceiling.

Party walls are made thicker than necessary. Their function is to shut out noise from the neighboring house and to stop fires spreading from the neighboring house. They are capable of supporting loads but they stand idle. Let us give them the ceilings to support and save ourselves the load-bearing walls. Let our joists go from party wall to party wall.

That would create hangars, open to the street and to the yard. Let us nail boards to the front and rear joists. Now the hangars are enclosed.

Openings for doors and windows can be sawn out.

A second layer of vertical boards is nailed to the window frames.

The pipes are run inside the hollow walls, which are then plastered over on the interior. On the exterior they are clad with weatherboarding. Now the hollow hanging walls are protected against wind and weather.

The houses the Americans live in from Florida to Alaska consist of such walls, which must not be filled in.

They are warm and durable. Washington's birthplace has been standing for two hundred years.

Why are my walls left hovering above the ground?

You save half the foundations.

In the interior any change (enlargement) of the rooms can easily be carried out.

The house can be repeatedly extended on the garden side by lengthening the party walls.

If there are houses there already, one can erect a new house with just *one* wall.

That is why it is called *The house with one wall.*

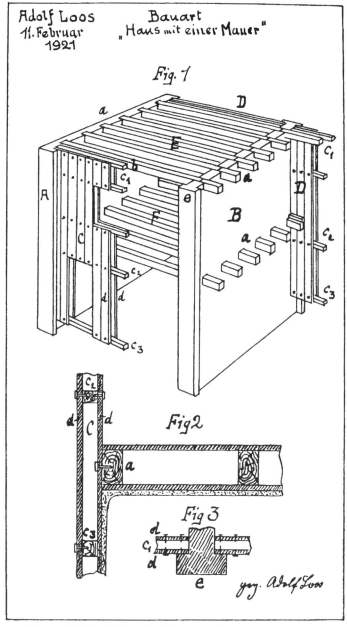

"House with One Wall" method of construction.

*

The purpose of this invention is to enable the construction of cheap dwelling houses or of buildings to be used as business/storage/factory premises or for agricultural, military or other functional purposes. The present high prices of all building materials, added to high wages plus the need for construction brought about by the shortage of housing all make any reduction in building costs a matter of urgency. This is especially true of housing for developments where low cost and rapid construction are prerequisites and long-term durability appears to be of secondary importance. Given the fixed nature of the price of land and of the costs of materials and labor, savings in building houses can only be made by a construction method which reduces the amount of materials and labor needed. This can be achieved by removing the necessity for a complete roof structure and a cellar. Beyond that, however, the present invention aims to make further savings in the foundations, which are always relatively expensive. In this new construction method they only need to be dug out for the two party walls. Thus the building method here submitted for a patent renders unnecessary the foundations for two façades as well as the erection of piers in those façades. This is done by hanging the front and rear walls instead of placing them, as at present, on supporting foundations.

The method is illustrated by:

Fig. 1: Elevation of a two-floor construction, without roof and foundations and with the façade partly cut away to reveal the interior.

Fig. 2: Section through the front and rear walls at the top of the first story.

Fig. 3: Section through the T-shaped part of the party wall at the façade.

Fig. 1 shows a housing unit with ground floor and second floor in the cheapest, self-contained type of building. The two party walls, A and B, stand on foundations with the joists, E and F, resting on them at points a, that is at ninety degrees to the usual direction they run from front to rear walls. This method means the front and rear walls, C and D, have no load to bear, making it possible to hang them without foundations. The front and rear walls, C and D in figs 1 and 2, consist of horizontal beams, C1, C2, C3 etc., to the interior and exterior of which is attached a casing of vertical boards, slats or shingles, d. The casing on the exterior must be sufficiently weathertight. For the best results the interior casing should be plastered. The gap between the inner and outer casings acts as heat insulation. This structure for the front and rear walls, in which door and windows are also indicated, is attached by beam C1, to joist d, with nails, bolts, cramp irons, iron angle or similar means. A further attachment of the wall to the ground floor joist, as indicated in fig. 2, is also recommended. From this it is clear that the front and rear walls are hung, do not need foundations and have no piers. Given this self-contained manner of building, once the first unit has been completed each of the adjoining houses uses the existing party wall of the neighboring house so that for each subsequent house only one wall with foundations has to be erected, for which reason the term "house with *one* wall" seems justified as a designation for this construction method. Recommended materials for cladding the hanging walls are: planks, asbestos or fibrocement tiles, asphalt-impregnated paper shingles, compressed waterproof and fireproof paper; for unheated buildings corrugated iron and sheet metal are also recommended.

It is also recommended that the ends of the party walls, where they join the front and rear walls, should be T-shaped, as shown in fig 3, thus making it easier to fit the hanging walls into the frontage and to seal them.

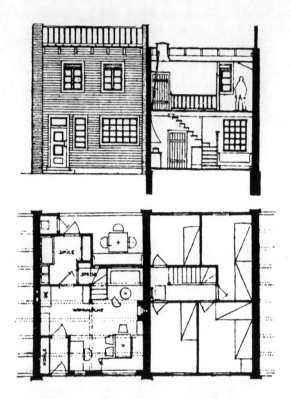

Projects for Row houses in Housing Developments. Ground plans, section and elevation of the street frontage of a 6-meter type (scale 1: 300).
Planned using the "house with one wall" construction method: the party walls alone bear both the joists, which run parallel to the street frontage, and the front and rear walls of the house which are simply hung between each pair of load-bearing walls.

31. Houses for the Lainz Social Housing Development (1921) ("To the Federal Housing and Development Fund")

On the Types of Houses

In judging this report we must start out from the question, "How can a detached house be cheaper than an apartment in a tenement?"

To Austrian ears that sounds paradoxical. So far all our experience here has shown that tenements work out cheaper. The common foundations, the common roof both seem to support the logic of Austrian experience. But in countries where for centuries individual houses have been the norm in cities as well as out in the country methods have been developed over the years which make our question understandable. Two elements of the structure of a detached house in particular have been fundamentally transformed: the staircase and the ceiling.

In a tenement the staircase, being open to all tenants, is a public passageway, in fact just a continuation of the sidewalk. What more natural, then, than to give it the same grade you often find on sidewalks and steps in hilly towns (Fischerstiege, Thurngasse)? If you have to go up several floors in an apartment house, you unconsciously calculate the exertion necessary and go up at a leisurely pace, floor by floor, using each step.

It is different when you are only heading for the mezzanine. Then you will observe that your nerves won't let you go up step by step. You take them two at a time, to get there as quickly as possible. A perfect example of this is the comfortable incline of the stairs to the top of the double-decker streetcars that are running on a trial basis from Eschenbachgasse to Hietzing.

How comfortable we find stairs is not something that can be measured in figures, then, but a matter of psychology and physiology. If I were to put a second set of stairs in the same streetcar with the familiar tenement gradient, the simple fact that these "comfortable" stairs were never used would make nonsense of the notion of "comfort."

The function of the stairs in a tenement is to separate the apartments from each other as much as possible. Stairs in a house have the opposite function, namely to connect the living area (ground floor) and sleeping area (second floor) as well as possible. That will be all the easier the less height there is to climb and the steeper the stairs. The maximum steepness will be limited by consideration for children and invalids. For this reason the English Ministry of Agriculture warns against making stairs too steep and suggests an incline of forty-five degrees with risers between 19.5 and 21.5 cm, since making it possible to get upstairs quickly (comfort!) has led to staircases in small English houses that are far too steep.

It is well known that in all countries where houses are commoner the stairs are so narrow that furniture has to be brought in through the window.

Houses in Holland, northern France and Belgium therefore have a pulley in the roof space. A staircase of 80 cm width is ample and allows easy passing. (People feel uncomfortable on steep stairs if they are too wide.)

The answer to the demand that the stairs be made wider so that "substantial pieces of furniture" such as wardrobes, sofas, pianos etc. can be carried up is that these experts have completely misunderstood the purpose of the upper floor. Firstly, the upper floor is for sleeping alone. Pianos etc. have no business there. (They will probably be forbidden by the regulations anyway since the party walls are not soundproof enough for pianos.) The inhabitants of these houses will not have free-standing wardrobes, but will use cheap built-in closets, which cost much less and reduce the amount of dusting necessary. Secondly, given the relatively low height of the upper floor, the occasional removal will be carried out most easily (and therefore cheaply) through the window.

It is of utmost importance for people living in tenements for the ceiling to be as deep as possible. They want as little sound as possible from their neighbors above and below to reach them. That the extra height involved means an increase in the height of the staircase is of no concern to them, since they live on one floor.

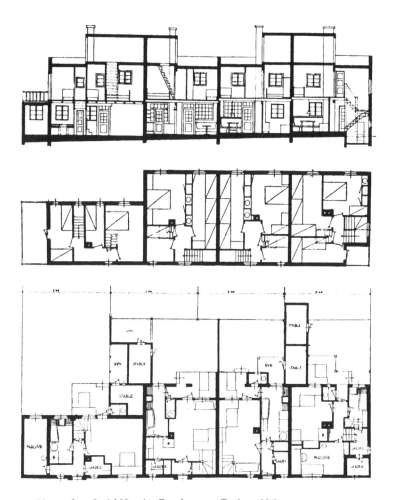

Houses for a Social Housing Development (Project 1921)
— longitudinal section
— upper-floor ground plan
— lower-floor ground plan

For people who live on two floors, however, the main thing is to have as shallow a ceiling structure as possible, since one step more or less makes a difference. That means no soundproofing; after all, it is your own family you can hear in the next room, in this case the room above. Father is upstairs and that's all there is to it. For that reason English houses have no layer of rubble between ceiling and floor (heat saving in low stories).

These three comfort factors — steep stairs, low ceiling height and no floor filling — are all the savings we can make in the houses for the project. If the state were to insist on the same building methods that quite justifiably obtain for tenements it would make the whole social housing movement in Austria impossible. I leave it to the public to decide whether it is appropriate, in a poor state such as Austria, deliberately to make house construction more expensive, while it would never occur to rich states like England to compel their citizens to squander their resources.

I regard the note about the placing of the WC (earth closet) on the first floor as a joke, or proof of complete ignorance of the real world. The houses submitted are to be sited on sloping ground. The entrance from the street is on the ground floor, the garden (the rear) is one storey lower. Naturally the WC is sited at garden level, in this case in the "cellar." In contrast to the traditional arrangement, which demands a separate outhouse, English regulations allow an earth closet to be placed under the same roof, provided the instructions regarding the spreading of peat are properly observed, though in general the entrance is not inside the house, but from outside.

English regulations also state that where the scullery is used for washing (clothes) it is recommended that it be separated from the living area by a vestibule. Compare with that the criticism of this arrangement by the ministry. Double boarding is provided for everywhere it is required because of smells or steam, that is over the stable, cellar and scullery. It is unnecessary in the living room as there is an extractor hood over the stove.

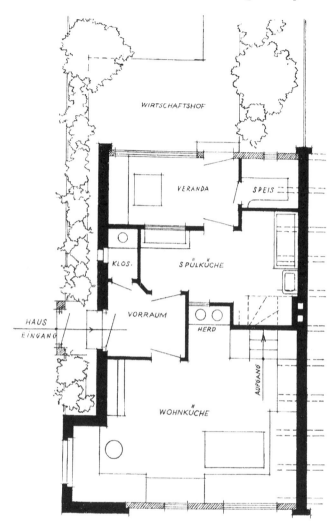

Project for Row Houses for Housing Project, 1920-1922. Corner type, ground plan (scale 1: 150); viewed from living room/kitchen, joists laid from party wall to party wall.
[words on plan, from top to bottom and left to right: yard; veranda; larder; toilet; scullery; entrance; vestibule; stove; stairs up; kitchen/living room].

Remarks on the Site Development Plan

The idea of creating a picturesque ensemble was deliberately abandoned. My guidelines were:
1. Economy of layout
2. Practical arrangement of the gardens for growing vegetables
3. Ease of approach from the Tiergarten entrance

1: The site is divided in two by a wide, straight avenue running east to west. For economic reasons this existing road, which has a good bed, if somewhat in need of repair, was not discarded but used in the site development plan. In order to preserve the woodland character it is so arranged that bands of trees are left, forty meters to the north of the road and twenty meters to the south, so that the gleam of the houses will be seen through the foliage. As well as that, the row of houses is set back in places to reduce the monotony of a continuous line of houses, which will be broken up by frequent corner houses. Given the length of the avenue, it was clear that an interruption was an aesthetic necessity. We needed to provide a culmination point for the woodland road, therefore a tall towerlike building was planned to be sited on this axis. It goes without saying that the best place for it is the highest point of the road. (The road rises gently then slopes down for the last fifth of its length, after the big meadow.) Nearby is the lower pond.

Not only economic but also aesthetic considerations suggest we should make this lower pond, which is surrounded by a wall of undressed stone, the social center of the project. The community building, sited on the banks of this pool with the rising woodland behind, would be reflected in the water, creating a delightful picture. The longitudinal axis of the pond does not run parallel to Hermesstraße. But the highest point of the site is perpendicular to the lateral axis of the pond. These considerations led to the proposal for an ornamental road from the community building to the top, which is to be crowned by a tower. There is economic justification for the necessary realignment of the small part of Hermesstraße from the school to the meadow in that it makes room for twenty-three houses. Moreover this new section of road fits in better with the contours, allowing Hermesstraße to enter the big meadow at a point six meters higher.

The great length of the gardens has been criticized. It would, of course, have been simple to have, instead of the row, double houses with double gaps between and to site another row of such houses on the existing southern road, making each garden twice as wide and half as long. But the consequence would be that all the mains (gas, water, electricity) would have to be laid to two rows of houses, while with the long gardens these costs are halved. This consideration holds not only for this one street, but for the whole site plan.

The Federal Ministry of Commerce, Trade, Industry and Building and Social Administration seems unencumbered by this sense of economic responsibility.

It is considered a mistake in the site development plan that the gardens are aligned north to south. "This means that one row of houses is permanently in the shade, the other constantly exposed to the sun's rays."

The house type presented here has the following rooms facing south: stable, workroom, garden-level WC, livingroom/kitchen, small room and parents' bedroom on the second floor, small double bedroom on the third floor. Facing north: cellar, scullery, small single bedroom. It goes without saying that the type for the row of houses opposite to be built next year will not be simply a mindless inverted copy of this one. The north-south alignment of the houses means that the west side, the side exposed to the weather, is avoided, which will do a great deal toward making annual repairs to the exterior plasterwork unnecessary. (After years of struggle, the owners of houses in the Lainz area have given up and clad the whole of the windward side with weatherproof boards or tiles which, with row houses, would be an aesthetic disaster.)

2: One important fact is that all experts in growing vegetables are unanimous in declaring that the most correct alignment for the garden is north-south.

It is correct that with long gardens ten percent goes on the path or paths. With a garden seven meters wide the beds are six meters long, a good size for the amateur gardener. Below is a breakdown of an area of five hundred square meters for two different shapes of plot: seven by seventy-one meters and twenty by twenty-five meters:

Long plot		Short plot after Garden Inspector Vogt	
Front garden			
3 m wide	21 m²	60m²	
House	42 m²	42 m²	
Yard behind house		Yard at side of house	
	42 m²	42 m²	
Paths	45 m²	67.50 m²	
Total	150 m²	211.50 m²	
Left for vegetables			
	350 m²	288.50 m²	

Thus with the arrangement so often requested by the lay public I would lose sixty-one-and-a-half square meters. I would also like to point out, moreover, that the row, with the houses abutting, means the yard is completely hidden from passers-by, giving the occupants the necessary feeling of privacy. Moreover, every owner of a detached house knows that the ground between the houses is of less use, because of the shade from the house.

It would be going too far to discuss the principles of modern gardening here in order to demonstrate why a garden should be aligned north-south (sunshine) and why it should be as long as possible (protection from the wind). Anyone who wants to go into this — and it is certainly to be recommended for the building expert assigned to the Ministry for Social Administration — can read up on it in Leberecht Migge.

3: A housing development that is planned from the point of view of the picturesque alone, and therefore takes no account of the occupants' nerves, is wrong.

Every inhabitant of the development can justifiably demand that his property be reached by the quickest route. Winding paths, twisting roads, zigzags, in short anything that takes the occupant away from his house, even for a short stretch, compelling him to go back the same distance (towards his house), should never be allowed for ornamental reasons, but only if the gradient is too steep for vehicles. The routes on my development plan are all so arranged that they are directed toward the Tiergarten entrance. The paths people make without thinking about it give the best routes. That is the way all roads (picturesque roads!) developed. The French curve is a worse danger than the T-square.

A footpath has been trodden from the Tiergarten entrance to the highest point of the site. This path is the first that is to be made up. Its course is retained. With a gradient of 50% perpendicular to the contour lines, it takes the most comfortable route to the top.

This gradient is comparable to the gradients in Vienna from the Ring to the western districts (Mariahilfer Straße, Lerchenfelderstraße, Burggasse). To take a path up such a slope by zigzags simply in order to avoid the direct route across the contours would amount to an assault on the nerves of someone who wants to get out of the snow or rain and reach the shelter of his home as quickly as possible.

The steep slope at the foot of the ornamental road (from the lower pond to the water tower) can be avoided if vehicles go to the houses at the top via the road that slants across the contours.

I would like to append a few aesthetic considerations. It is not the rectilinear plan that makes the new housing developments in Hietzing and the Cottage district so dreary, but the fact that all the streets have the same character. This mistake has been avoided in my site plan. Every road has its own character. Hermesstraße is bordered by woodland on both sides. The next road has a twenty-meter-wide strip of woodland in the middle, houses on both sides. The road after that has houses on one side only, the other has gardens. It is not until the next but one that there are houses on both sides again.

This arrangement means that each road has an individual look and thus, despite the similar types of house, will not be mistaken for the others — a result that would not be achieved by having winding roads.

32. Social Housing Development Day (1921)

The food of a nation is determined by the produce of its land under cultivation. Every nation, therefore, has its own type of food, its own cuisine.

The term "Austrian cuisine" was frequently used. It is only now, however, that we have come to realize that this cuisine was made possible by the fact that a combination of states known as the Austro-Hungarian monarchy lasted for centuries.

Our flour came from Moravia, Poland and Hungary, plums from southern Hungary, sugar from Bohemia and Moravia. Nature had lavished her riches on the non-German territories. Wide plains, black soil, burning heat. Now we have lost everything that once fed us. That means we have to readjust. We must create our own national cuisine. Bohemian *Knödel*, Moravian *Buchteln*,[1] Italian *Schnitzel (frittura)*, things which for centuries formed the basics of Viennese cuisine, will have to be replaced with indigenous food.

The wealth of flour produced by the old monarchy meant that Austrian cuisine was the most flour-rich of the whole world. Not for nothing were our desserts known as "flour dishes" (*Mehlspeisen*) and we were proud of them. Flour was added to every dish. No vegetables were served without a goodly amount of flour being mixed in. Housewives called that "stretching," for vegetables were expensive, flour cheap. Thus spinach in Austria was a gray paste which an admixture of spinach gave a greenish tinge. But now this extravagance is costing the nation twenty-five billion a year, the sum the state has to lay out for the flour we import from abroad. There is nothing our industry can do, however hard it tries, to produce sufficient exports to balance out this wanton import. Is there no way out? Who can save us from financial collapse?

***

Seventy years ago a man called Dr. Daniel Gottlieb Moritz Schreber died in Leipzig. He had seen children playing in the busy streets lined with tenements and thought, "Large families should get together to lease a patch of land outside the city gates where the children can play every day, out in the open, in fresh air and sunshine, far from the hurly-burly and dust of the city. An adult to supervise them should be provided by a different family each day. This patch of ground could be surrounded by summerhouses where father and mother could spend their leisure time after they had finished work."

And that is what happened. But a primal human instinct was aroused. The father saw the free, uncultivated ground. He who, during the day, was compelled by the division of labor to do constructive work alone felt a need for destructive labor. Every human activity consists of destroying and constructing. The joiner takes the wood, destroys it with chisel and plane, and then proceeds to construct the piece of furniture. The locksmith has to take up his file before he can think of putting together an object. People can live if their only activity is destruction, for that is the primal instinct. Children have the urge to destroy their toys, and the eternal child among men, the one whose sole activity is destruction, who never thinks of construction, whose only endeavor is to wound Mother Earth with pick and shovel, the miner, quite rightly bathes in the glory the German people and their writers have given him.

But people who, because of the division of labor, are compelled to perform constructive tasks alone, become stunted. They lose their humanity. Work becomes a terrible drudgery. Do not laugh at the bricklayer who, year in, year out, has to lay bricks and who, the moment the midday bell rings, cleans the mortar he has just spread off the brick and puts it down again. No midday gun would make this same man break off in the middle of a destructive activity and leave the spade stuck in the ground. And no mocking glance will greet him when he is the last to come to the canteen.

***

The father saw the free, uncultivated ground and although he had worked all day in the factory until he was weary, he took up his spade and began to dig over the land. In place of Dr. Schreber's children's playgrounds came tilled land. Wives and children helped, and thus what we today call the *Schrebergarten* came into being. It is wrong to attribute the *Schrebergarten* to Dr. Schreber. It did not spring from the mind of a single individual. It arose, as all necessary things arise, from a deep psychological need. It is the product of a revolution of the workers against the barracks-like constraint of the factory system, the product of a revolution that was bloodless and therefore had a humane outcome, in contrast to the bloody revolution forced on us by the inhumane tape measure.

Do not think that these allotments are a momentary craze. For all time to come the patch of ground people can cultivate for themselves will remain what it is today, their refuge with Mother Nature, their true happiness and supreme bliss.

***

It is the duty of the legislator to direct this craze into the right channels. His task is to see that this work, which part of the population undertake of their own free will, is put to the best use for society as a whole. The work of the allotment-holder produces food which would otherwise have to be imported from abroad. During the past year Vienna's allotments produced food to the value of a hundred million. The question the legislator must ask himself is, "How can this sum be increased in order to reduce the amount of food bought from abroad?"

There are two ways of achieving this. The first is to allocate land to anyone who is willing to undertake voluntarily the work necessary to produce food. There are hundreds of thousands in Vienna, millions in Austria who feel the urge to do gardening in their leisure time and whose desire and capacity to work are not being exploited. "Eight hours to work, eight hours to play, eight hours to rest, eight shillings a day," is the slogan of the English trade unions. Some of our workers want to invest their eight hours of play in profitable labor. The objection that these eight hours will be lost to regular work because workers will overexert themselves in their gardens and waste their strength on them is wrong. The opposite is true. This garden work is a first-class tonic. Presumably I do not need to elaborate on how these eight hours of play would otherwise be spent.

The allotment that is a long way away from where the gardener lives is a drain on time. Some take an hour by streetcar there and an hour back. Therefore we must turn as quickly as possible to the second way. Every allotment-holder should live where his garden is. In that way all members of the household can work in the garden during the day. Morning work, which is so important for the garden, could be done, all the garbage, kitchen waste and sewage could be used to improve the soil. For the same amount of time with which Vienna's allotment-holders made a billion, our owner-occupiers could make five times as much in a few years time — that is how long it will take to prepare the ground — from their gardens.

This is the point at which we could see a significant change in working practices. The worker who possesses neither home nor garden, the Viennese worker, that is (for who would call a worker's apartment in a Viennese tenement a home?), tries to spread his eight hours of "play" as far as possible over the whole working day by means of breaks. That is uneconomical. The owner of a house with garden will be the pioneer of the undivided working day. He will endeavor to get to work as late as possible and back to his garden as early as possible.

His home will be a source of joy. He will have a table at home around which the family can gather, as has the poorest cottager, the poorest woodcutter. Does the world know that there is a metropolis where eighty percent of its million inhabitants cannot eat their meals at a table?

On the table that is to be given to the Viennese worker will appear meals that represent the new, modern, truly Austrian cuisine. His wife will no longer need to "stretch" vegetables. Intensive cultivation of the soil, yielding three harvests per year, will result in the kind of diet which other civilized nations have long enjoyed, in contrast to those nations which can only count on one harvest a year. Vegetables raised in people's own garden will replace flour. What we lack in fertile soil we will make up by labor.

Tomorrow those who take part in this movement will march along the Ring. Silent and solemn, they will march behind their two symbols: the spade which destroys the earth and the spirit level which builds their houses. It will be the parade of an army of volunteer workers. To join them is a heroic decision. They are resolved to devote their eight hours of leisure on weekdays and the whole of their Sundays and holidays to rebuilding the country. They are resolved to shut themselves off from the inn and the café, from the bandstand on Sunday afternoons and from all their well-loved Viennese habits. No longer will the Sunday sunshine tempt them out on an excursion into the most beautiful countryside surrounding any metropolis. The garden calls and demands its tribute of labor, the more the sun blazes down. Doff your hats, citizens of Vienna, and bow. Look up to these men, women and children.

Notes

1. *Knödel* — dumplings; *Buchteln* — small yeast buns with a sweet filling.

33. Learning a New Way of Living (1921)

The new movement for housing developments with gardens, which has stricken all the inhabitants of this city like a fever, demands new people. People who, as that great gardener, Leberecht Migge, so rightly says, have modern nerves.

It is easy to describe a person with modern nerves. It makes no great demands on our imagination, since they already exist, though not in Austria but a little farther to the west. The nerves the Americans have today will be those our descendants have tomorrow.

In America there is not such a sharp division between town and country folk as here. Every countryman is half a city-dweller, every city-dweller half a countryman. American towns-people have not moved as far away from nature as their European counterparts or, to be more precise, their continental counterparts. The Englishman is also a real countryman.

Both, the Americans and the English, find sharing a roof with others a disagreeable situation. Everyone, rich or poor, endeavors to get their own home, even if it is only a cottage, a tumbledown shack with a sagging thatched roof. And in the cities they make believe and build tenements with individual apartments on two floors connected by a wooden staircase. Cottages stuck one on top of the other.

And now I come to the first point in my program. People living in their own home live on two floors. Their lives are sharply divided into two parts: life during the day and life at night, living and sleeping.

Do not imagine living on two floors is uncomfortable. True, the bedrooms are not what we would call bedrooms, they are too small and spartan for that. The only piece of furniture is a bedstead of brass or iron painted white. You won't even find a bedside table. and certainly not a wardrobe. It is replaced by the closet, a built-in wardrobe. These bedrooms are only used for sleeping. They are easy to keep tidy. There is one advantage they have over our bedrooms: they have only one door and thus cannot be used as passages. In the morning all members of the family come downstairs at the same time. The baby is brought down too and spends the day with its mother in the living area.

Every family has a table round which the whole family can gather for meals. Just like country folk. In Vienna only twenty percent of the population can do that. So what do the other eighty percent do? Well, one sits by the stove, another holds a pan in his hand, three are at the table, the rest occupy the windowledges.

And now every family that moves into a home of their own is to be given a table which, like the country folk, they keep in a corner of the living room. Like country folk. That will be a revolution! One can hear voices for and against. "Not us, no way. I've seen the peasants in Upper Austria. They sit round the table and all eat out of the same bowl. We don't do that! We have our own plates." And one worried father said, "What? Round a table? And let my children get into alehouse habits?"

When I tell people this, they laugh, but inwardly I cry.

We won't quarrel about the table. People will soon realize that breakfasting together saves money. Our Viennese breakfast — a mouthful of coffee standing beside the stove and a piece of bread that is eaten half on the stairs and half out in the street — demands something to fool the stomach at ten o'clock, a goulash, and the goulash, since it is well spiced with paprika, demands a glass of beer. We call this meal, for which the English and Americans do not even have a name, *Gabelfrühstück*, a "fork breakfast," probably because only the knife is used. One is not supposed to eat with one's knife, but, "What are you going to eat up the gravy with, then?"

We do not begrudge the father this second breakfast, as long as he has to make do with a mouthful of black coffee at home. But his wife will soon realize that for the same outlay the whole family could have a magnificent American breakfast which is so filling one has no room for anything else until midday. In American families breakfast is the best meal. Everyone is refreshed from their night's rest, the room is cozy, well aired and warm. The whole table is covered with food. First everyone eats an apple, the the mother gives everyone a helping of oatmeal, that marvelous dish to which America owes its energetic people, its greatness and well-being. The Viennese, however, will look glum at the idea of eating oats. But we will give the visitors who come out to Lainz porridge prepared in the American style and hope that we can convert the whole of Vienna into oat-eaters. We are proud of all those fine horses we feed our oats to, but what use are they? Our people, too, should be "glossy coated" and "well muscled-up."

Rich or poor, farmworker or millionaire, oatmeal is on everyone's breakfast table in America. Everything else, cheap fish or expensive veal cutlets, depends on their financial situation. Of course there is also tea and bread which, strangely enough, is also served at lunch and at the dinnertime.

Lunch is very simple. Father is out, mother has been busy all morning doing the housework, for housewives don't have servants. And this absence of servants has led to food being prepared in the living room. The woman of the house has a right to spend her time in the living room and not in the kitchen.

This arrangement leads to the cooking work being divided into two sharply separated parts. One is the work at the stove, the other the initial preparation and the dish-washing. The first part is carried out in the living room, which is where the stove is situated. This does make it necessary to conceal the stove as far as possible from the view of the other occupants.

It is incredible how many things have been invented in America to solve this problem! Only recently I saw a photograph in a magazine, two photographs, to be exact. One showed a stove in an alcove, the other a desk. It was the same alcove. Just press the button and the whole thing, powered by electricity, revolves.

But this arrangement demands more than mere technology can provide. It demands people who are not afraid of cooking. We who, unlike country folk and the English and Americans, feel mild disgust at the sight of cooking, are astonished that these exotic nations have restaurants in their hotels where the cooking is carried out in full view of the diners. During the war we invented a German name for them, but now we call them grill rooms again. But the simple worker in his house in the housing development will call it his "kitchen/living room" or "cooking room" and eat just like an English lord. Or an Austrian peasant.

Anyone who wants to join the house-and-garden project will have to adapt. We must forget the inhabitant of the city tenement. If we want to go out into the country we must learn from the country folk and see how they do things. We will have to learn a new way of living.

34. The Chicago Tribune Column (1923)

In producing this design the author constantly bore in mind the demand in the prospectus "to erect the most beautiful and distinctive office building in the world," to erect a building that once seen, either in a photograph or in reality, can never be forgotten, to raise a monument that will forever be associated with the image of the city of Chicago, just as the dome of St Peter's is with Rome and the leaning tower with Pisa, to design a building that for the intelligentsia will immediately connect the newspaper, *The Chicago Tribune*, with a particular character.

How to achieve this? By erecting the highest building in the world, higher than the Woolworth Building? The restriction on height to 400 feet made this impossible. By repeating the trick of the New York Herald or the Morgan Building and making it lower than the surrounding buildings? Such imitation would run counter to the competition requirements. Or by choosing new architectural forms without tradition, such as German, Austrian and French architects use, forms from the Berlin of Cubism or the Belgium of the 1848 revolution? Alas, all these untraditional forms are all too quickly replaced by new ones and the owner soon realizes his building is old-fashioned because these forms change as fast as ladies' hats.

There seemed to be nothing for it, then, but to design the typical American skyscraper. When this movement started it was easy to distinguish between them, but already the non-specialist finds it difficult to say whether the building whose photograph he is looking at is in San Francisco or Detroit.

For his design, therefore, the author chose the column. There are precedents in the tradition for the concept of a huge, free-standing column: the Column of Trajan was the model for Napoleon's column on Place Vendôme.

I was immediately assailed by architectural and aesthetic reservations. Is it permissible to build an inhabited column? To that one must answer that precisely the most beautiful designs for skyscrapers have been taken from monuments that were not intended for habitation and no one has yet objected to them for

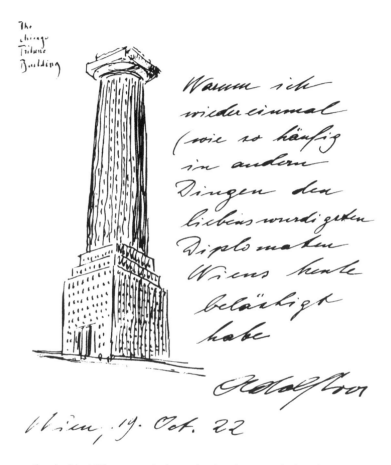

[handwriting] Why once again (as so often in other matters) I have been pestering the most charming diplomat in Vienna — Adolf Loos — Vienna, Oct. 19, 1922.

Competition entry for a palatial newspaper building for the Chicago Tribune, 1922.
Dedication to Legationstrat Dr. Peterka.
Werner J. Schweiger Archive, Vienna.

that reason. For example the classical model of the tomb of King Mausolus for the Metropolitan Building and the model of the Gothic spire for the Woolworth Building.

You can rest assured that despite this I found it difficult to bring myself to publish my idea. There are people who, given the Catonian severity for which I have made a name for myself, would claim I was betraying my principles in doing something they would quite happily accept from any other architect. I will state here and now that I have not betrayed my principles and stand by my design unconditionally. With my close connections with the newspaper business, being not only an architect but also a writer and contributor to all modern art journals, and having worked in my younger days as art critic in New York, I am well aware how far one can go, in terms of architecture, with a newspaper building. This design is worthy of a *Chicago Tribune*, for a small newspaper it would be presumptuous.

Most objections, I fear, will be directed at the lack of decoration in my project. This building is intended as a gigantic demonstration of my doctrine that we replace the ornamentation of antiquity with the quality of our materials. It is to be made of one material alone: *black, polished granite.*

No illustration is capable of revealing the effect of this column. The smooth, polished surfaces of the cubic base and the fluting of the column would make an overwhelming impression on the observer. It would be a surprise, a sensation even in these modern and blasé times.

The building is no higher than the regulations allow, but the perspective created by the abacus makes it *appear* higher.

I have been lavish in the use of space. Monumentality is always achieved at the cost of space: high entrance halls, broad staircases etc. The owner must remember that true grandeur is not characterized by petty utility but that the most impressive effects are obtained by the opposite, as is proved by the New York Herald Building and the Morgan Building.

The return between the base of the column and the plant building is to be of brick and terracotta, with the exception of the cornice and the columns, which are to be of the same material as the main building. This will be the best way of showing that the new building and the existing plant belong together.

The colossi over the entrance columns have their antecedent in tradition in the Temple of Jupiter at Acragas and in the crouching figure in the Theater of Dionysos in Athens.

If the height restriction of four hundred feet should be removed the statue of a seated Roman tribune could be placed on top of the column.

Until now huge columns have only been erected in the Roman style, never the Greek. Until now this idea was slumbering in our imagination, now it has taken on form.

This huge, Greek Doric column will be built. If not in Chicago, then in another city. If not for the Chicago Tribune, *then for someone else. If not by me, then by another architect.*

35. Grand Babylon Hotel (1923)

Ten years ago I built the villa for Dr. Gustav Scheu in Hietzing on the outskirts of Vienna. The general response was a shaking of heads. People thought that type of building might be appropriate for Algiers, but not for Vienna. When designing the house I did not have the Orient in mind at all. I just thought it would be very convenient to be able to step out from the bedrooms, which were on the second floor, onto a large, communal terrace. Anywhere, in Algiers as well as Vienna. This terrace, then, which was repeated on the third floor (an apartment that was rented out), was the unusual, exceptional feature. A member of the city council tabled a formal question demanding that the city building department ban buildings of this type.

The question is: why for thousands of years have terraces been usual in the Orient and why are they not used in our latitudes? The answer is simple. With the construction methods available until now flat roofs and roof terraces could only be built in frost-free regions.

The invention of the Häusler-type roof cladding and the use of asphalt have made the flat roof, and therefore the terrace, possible. For four centuries the flat roof has been the dream of architects. In the middle of the nineteenth century this dream was realized. But most architects did not know what to do with the flat roof. Today one can say that the flat roof, as the best, cheapest and most durable roof, is the criterion by which one can tell whether one is dealing with an architect or a stage designer.

I have always longed to build this kind of terraced house for workers' homes. The fate of proletarian children from the first year of their lives to the time they go to school seems particularly harsh to me. A communal terrace, allowing supervision to be shared out among neighbors, would release children from the prison of the apartments where they are locked in. When the Paris autumn *Salon* invited me to exhibit my works I was faced with the choice between showing a project for one of these terraced workers' houses or one for a terraced hotel. The latter

is much more effective in terms of propaganda. There is a widely read novel by Arnold Bennett, *Grand Babylon Hotel.* I had my name.

Every hotel has to be designed to meet the needs of the place where it is situated. I decided on the Riviera, which I knew very well. But every hotel must also be designed to meet the needs of a particular social class. Inadequacies in buildings make the fulfillment of these demands impossible. Even in a luxury hotel dark rooms giving onto a yard have to be let at low rates. My terraced hotel has no rooms looking out onto the yard. Moreover the projecting construction means the sunny sides, the east and west sides, are lengthened. The most important aspect, however, is that each room has a terrace in front. Only the vertical northern wing lacks it. the length and breadth of this wing make it possible to use the roof area as an airplane station.

If we liken the project to two coupled pyramids, we can talk of two gigantic burial chambers, the heart of the pyramids. One burial chamber will be made into a palatial skating rink, the other into a great banqueting hall and ballroom. Between the two pyramids is a hall lit from above which, in place of a glass roof, which would look unsightly from the inner terraces, will have a pool with a Lux-glass bottom.

The hotel could be built, if the proposed site could be secured. The fifty retail premises, some of which are inside the hotel, some on the street frontage, would, given the extraordinary level of rent usual there, secure a return of five percent, independent of the the hotel business and all other enterprises. It is presumably a justified assumption that a hotel with a thousand beds would also bring in a reasonable return.

36. Furnishing a Modern Apartment (1924)
(The Abolition of Furniture)

My friends, let me tell you a secret.
There is no such thing as modern furniture!

Or, to be more exact, *only furniture that is movable can be modern.* All other pieces of "furniture" which have their permanent place against the wall, that is, are not movable, that is are not proper pieces of furniture, pieces such as chests and wardrobes, display cabinets and sideboards, no longer exist.

People didn't realize that. That was what led to all the mistakes. People said that every period had made its modern, up-to-date wardrobes and sideboards and all we had to do was make our own up-to-date versions. There was a flaw in their logic. Since there are no such things as wardrobes anymore, we cannot create modern ones. The function of these pieces of furniture is storage. The china was kept in the sideboard, clothes in the wardrobe. Having special pieces of furniture for storing things was a sign of an elegant lifestyle. Chests and cupboards were a family's way of flaunting their wealth to visitors. A sideboard would contain all the family's glass, china and silver. It was magnificent. A resplendent high altar in the best position in the dining room and in the holy of holies, the tabernacle, stood the brandy glasses. I always used to say to my pupils, "The more vulgar the family, the bigger and more richly adorned the sideboard. Emperors have none at all."

Anxiously, the housewife who is not up-to-date will ask where she is supposed to put all these things? But there is a mass of empty wall space, window embrasures and alcoves along the route from kitchen to dining room which, closed off with a softwood door, would make a much more practical facility for storing glasses and china than the deep sideboard. Glasses and plates should not be kept behind each other.

Even less up-to-date is keeping our clothes in wardrobes which are used as splendid showpieces in the room. Remember, a wardrobe is really like a case for a valuable piece of jewelry.

Now just consider the discrepancy between the receptacle — the wardrobe — and our modern clothes. The wardrobe is covered in carving and inlay, our clothes are plain. There was a connection between a French courtier's *armoire* and his clothes with their diamond buttons. And it was part of the spirit of the age to show off with wardrobes and cupboards and to let the rich decoration of the wardrobe suggest the costliness of its contents. But, to be honest, my friends, would you not find such behavior in a person of today vulgarly brazen?

Architects too — I mean modern architects — ought to be people of today, that is modern people. If they were there would be no applied art, no "art in the service of commerce." It is based on a misunderstanding. Because Dürer designed clothes and shoes, Holbein jewelry, today's artists think they must do the same. But being a modern person means you know you can leave that to the shoemaker and tailor, to the gem-setter and pearl-dealer.

And movable furniture can be left to the cabinetmaker and decorator. They make magnificent pieces of furniture. Modern pieces of furniture, furniture that is as modern as our shoes and clothes, as our leather suitcases and automobiles. Of course, this means you can't show off with your trousers anymore and say, "These are from the Bauhaus in Weimar."

People who are not modern today are an insignificant minority. Most of them are architects. They are artificially cultured at schools of applied art. It is a funny thing to do, in these modern days, to bring people up to the level of past times, but one should not laugh. It has done much damage.

What should the modern architect do?

He should build houses where all these pieces of "furniture" which are not movable, pieces which, I maintain, do not exist today, vanish into the walls. Whether he is building a new house or just doing the interior decoration for an old one.

If the architects had always been modern men, then all our houses would have built-in wardrobes and cupboards. The English built-in wardrobe is centuries old. Until the 1870s houses in France had built-in wardrobes. But the false revival of cupboard architecture has led to the disappearance of this modern feature. Today even in Paris they only build houses without built-in wardrobes.

Brass bedsteads, iron bedsteads, tables and dining chairs, easy chairs, occasional chairs and tables, all things which our crafts-men — never our architects — make in the modern manner, the householder should buy as required, following his own taste and inclination. Everything will go with everything else because they are all modern (just as my shoes go with my suit, my hat, my tie and my umbrella, even though the craftsmen involved do not know each other).

But the walls belong to the architect.

Here he is master of his own world. And with the walls go the non-movable pieces of furniture. They must not look like furniture. They are part of the wall and do not have the indepen-dent existence of the old-fashioned ornamental cupboards.

37. On Thrift (1924) (Excerpt)

If someone says to me it must be a cruel punishment to be condemned to live in one of the usual prisons, whose plainness, whitewashed walls and wooden bed make it seem pleasant, then I don't know how much more dreadful being imprisoned in one of the latest interiors would be, created by a "modern architect" from carpets to curtains, from ashtray to clock face and from coal scuttle to inkstand.

Ten years in prison for such a designer!

Our architects — furniture designers and interior decorators — see their main task as overtaking. Yes, overtaking. A shoemaker who makes good shoes can never do better than make his good shoes. And if I make his products last, because I have lots of pairs of shoes, they will always be modern. Shoemakers don't try to overtake each other, thank God. And God forbid architects should design shoes. Then our shoemakers would be desperately trying to overtake each other every two years.

I have had shoes for twenty years and they have never gone out of fashion.

I do not need to draw my designs. A good architectural concept of how something is to be built can be written down. The Parthenon can be written down.

I am against photographing interiors. The results are always different from the original. There are architects who design interiors not so people can live in them, but so they will look beautiful in the photographs. These are so-called drawing-board designs which, with their mechanical combination of light and shade, correspond most to a piece of mechanical equipment, in this case the darkroom. My interiors cannot be judged from photographs or reproductions. I am sure that in photographs they will look wretched, make no impression at all.

Photographs *dematerialize* reality, but precisely what I want is for people in my rooms to feel the material around them, I want it to have its effect on them, I want them to be aware of the enclosing room, to feel the material, the wood, to see it, touch it, to perceive it sensually, to sit comfortably and feel the contact between the chair and a large area of their peripheral sense of touch, and say: this is sitting as it should be. How can I demonstrate on a photograph how good my chairs are to sit on? How can I make a person who sees the photograph feel it, however well the chair is photographed?

So you see, photography says nothing. Photography produces pretty or not so pretty pictures. It diverts people from the real object, miseducates them. It is photography's fault that people want to furnish their rooms not for living in but to look nice. Photography is a deceiver. I have never tried to deceive anyone with my things. It is a method I condemn. But our architects have been educated in this method of deception alone and develop out of it. They make their reputation with pretty drawings and beautiful photographs. They do it deliberately, for they know that people are so clueless that a graphic, a photographic illusion is sufficient to get them to live in the interior and even be proud of it. And the clients are so dishonest they refuse to admit even to themselves that they can only live among all these drawings and photographs at the cost of self-denial.

— Folk art? What is it? Bare knees? Folk costumes? Folk dances? And we people from the city are supposed to go and look at it as if we were sitting in the theater? Is that not nonsense? Is it not as humiliating for us as it is for the country folk? Do we city-dwellers need it any more than those who live in the country?

The barriers between town and country ought to disappear anyway. The difference is artificial and therefore ridiculous. We regard country people as primitive. We laugh at them. They laugh at us. We should be ashamed of this artificial barrier, this lack of understanding of basic functions, the lack of understanding of people's work, of the higher mission any worker has, whatever their useful task, wherever they live, in Paris or the most out-of-the-way village in Moravia. Two such people may have their significant qualities, the Moravian does not have to be useless as a human being and the Parisian can be a complete idiot, or one of them could be something and the other nothing; the important thing is that the mere fact that a person lives on a particular spot on the globe and does this or that work makes absolutely no difference to their humanity. Only a blinkered person from Prague or Vienna can imagine he is better than someone who lives and works in Jihlava or Lhota.

I am always happy when I have spent some time in America and England.

An English bride would most of all like to take her parents' furniture with her. Here in Vienna brides are deaf to the suggestion that they would make things easier financially for their parents if they took over some of their furniture. They want to have something new, "fashionable," "modern." They even want something "artist-designed." And in four years' time they will want another "artist-designed" interior because they think their furniture is no longer modern and now there are new "artist-designed interiors." That is terrible! That is a waste of energy, labor, money and does tremendous damage to our economy.

And English furniture is the peak of comfort as well, while ours — "artist-designed by leading architects" — is a pyramid of nonsense and sins against the material, function and workmanship.

An English club chair is an absolutely perfect thing. In England and America there are many such perfect models among other types of furniture. I believe that each year only one good model capable of lasting any length of time is made. Everything else disappears within a few years, people soon find it as impossible as an old hat. The products of our so-called applied art are lame, and "artist-designed" furnishings only exist because they are commissioned and paid for in advance, because they have been produced anyway, because this unique ensemble is there in the apartment and people have to put up with it whether they like it or not — if they have made the mistake of ordering it in the first place.

This is why I don't like people referring to me as "the architect Adolf Loos." Plain "Adolf Loos" is my name.

Truly, the Viennese have something against economizing. It

is a real mania, the way they are constantly changing their apartments, acquiring something new, rearranging things, dashing from one architect to another. This chaos is a sign of our times and anyone who can help bring a little calm to our architecture will be doing a public service.

We do not have architecture, we have houses that are dressed up. As if one were to say, "This is not a saddle, but a dressed-up saddle." That is, a saddle with an ornamental form whose function is completely or at least substantially concealed beneath the "applied-art" dress, like the female body in a designer "applied-art" dress. At least we have to put on clothes, but why we have to dress up our architecture is something I cannot understand.

If the Ring in Vienna were to be built today instead of in the 1870s we would have a complete architectural disaster. There is only one thing I ask of an architect: that his building should have dignity.

Whenever I was in Brno and saw the *Deutsches Haus* and the Czech Beseda[1] the character of these two buildings told me how things would eventually turn out in Brno. It's obvious! I would like to reproduce these two pictures next to each other somewhere. But after what I recently saw in Prague I think Czech architects have been converted to the form of the Deutsches Haus in Brno. It is a bad sign.

One millimeter more or less on a molding is something that pains me. By nature and education today's architects are not thrifty people, to say nothing of those who go in for stage décor, from whom nothing sensible can be expected. These are people for whom *not* economizing on materials has become a set habit. They become specialists in papier mâché rocks, in all sorts of tricks and illusions, and completely lose any sense of proportion because that is the only way to do it in the theater: everything is done so casually, all that matters is the way it looks. Theater directors have invited me to productions of plays. I did not go. It went against my whole nature. I find theater architecture unbearable. It is not architecture at all.

Whether something is modern or not can best be decided by

seeing if it looks in place alongside old furniture. I assure you that my furniture looks in place alongside European furniture of all centuries and countries and fits in no less well with Chinese, Japanese and Indian objects. I challenge anyone to try that with the products of our so-called applied art!

The first thing in a room is the chair. If I am furnishing a room I must have a chair first and from that I go on to everything else.

I believe it is a great mistake for people to acquire pieces of furniture made of fine woods and costly fabrics. They will have to keep a permanent eye open to make sure nothing is damaged. There are all kinds of materials for real rooms, even if only pigskin, oak, wool.

An apartment must never be completed. Are we human beings ever finished, complete in our physical and psychological development? Do we ever come to a standstill? And if a human being is in constant movement and development, if old needs disappear and new ones arise, if Nature as a whole and everything around us is always changing, should the thing that is closest to a human being, his home, remain unchanged, dead, furnished for all time? No. It is ridiculous to lay down to people where a thing should stand, design everything for them from the lavatory pan to the ashtray. On the contrary, I like people to move their furniture round so that it suits them (not me!), and it is quite natural (and I approve) when they bring the old pictures and mementos they have come to love into a new interior, irrespective of whether they are in good taste or bad. That is not at all important to me, but for them they are charged with emotion and intimacy. That is to say, I am an architect who designs his interiors from a human perspective and not from an inhuman artistic one. I am astonished how many people let themselves be tyrannized by so-called "architects for interior design."

The motto for the training our architects receive at the academies is, "The way things used to be is not the way for today." I went through it as well. It took years of torment to get that useless training out of my system, to retrain myself until I came to understand that in one respect the aristocrat should serve as a model to us all. I mean in his sense of material. Not just any old horse, not even a beautiful horse, but a thoroughbred horse, even if it looked less pretty. Not any old suitcase but one made of the very best material. A solid one, made to last for centuries. And so I came to see the rightness of the principle followed by many an intellectually otherwise rather limited member of the Jockey Club. The sole important factors for aristocrats are the materials and perfect workmanship. All this was a difficult process for me. Why? Because people felt it was shameful to say that was what was right. It is Ruskin, by the way, who is to blame for all this. I am his sworn enemy. At some time in 1895, while I was in America, I came to realize that a Thonet chair was the most modern chair there is.

Any cabinetmaker can make the objects I use for my interiors. I am not an architect who wants to patent his ideas. Any craftsman in marble or textiles, any manufacturer can make my things and they do not have to beg my permission. The main thing is that he does honest work. And there is nothing I have avoided in my life so much as producing new forms.

Architects are there to get to the bottom of life, to think through people's needs to the very end, to help the disadvantaged in our society and to equip as large a number of households as possible with perfect objects of everyday use. Architects are not there to invent new forms.

But you can count the number of people in Europe today who will understand these views on the fingers of one hand.

Notes

1. "Club (house)": the premises of a Czech nationalist organization, as the Deutsches Haus was for the Germans.

38. Josef Veillich (1929)

Old Veillich is dead. He was buried yesterday.

Anyone who knows me knows who I mean. Any client of mine will have met him. His death will bring about a great change in our homes. To explain that I need to digress a little.

It is well known that all this artistic posturing in interior design — in all countries — doesn't impress anyone; that the whole hullabaloo, with its associations, schools, professorships, journals, exhibitions etc. has provided no new stimulus; that the whole development of modern craftwork, as far as it has not been influenced by inventions, comes from one pair of eyes. And those are mine.

In fact, it's not known at all, and I'm not going to wait for my obituary. I'm going to say it myself.

I am well aware of the outrage these lines will cause, if they should appear in print during my lifetime. But, my dear reader, can you remember what furniture and interiors you were expected to put up with in recent years? Has not everything which is ten years old become as aesthetically impossible (you would call is out-of-date) as a lady's hat? "Just look at that rubbish, I did it three years ago," said the modern architect and for that remark was celebrated as the great man who can outgrow himself every year. No craftsman would be capable of saying anything like that. With such an attitude one marks oneself down as an artist.

It will be different when people can distinguish clearly between art and craft, when the confidence tricksters and barbarians have been driven out of the temple of art. In a word, when my mission has been fulfilled.

As you can see, it has been a long road.

Stages:

Invited to take part in a *Sezession* craft exhibition, I replied, "I will only exhibit if suitcases by Würzl and clothes by Frankl are included in the exhibition." Outrage. But in Paris three years ago there were among the "art objects" some which took playfulness to excess. (Incidentally, Viennese Philistines also indulge

their "play instinct" — the latest excuse of our applied artists —
by playing cards, but none of them expects society to pay them
for the time they spend doing it.) So, there in the middle of these
excesses of "fine work" were some suitcases by a respectable
manufacturer of leather goods which, however, showed divergences from the correct form which would make any owner
embarrassed to give them to the hotel porter to carry. But
without these divergences they would not have been accepted for
the exhibition.

In the year the *Wiener Werkstätte* was founded:[1]

I said, "That you have a certain talent one cannot deny, but
it lies in quite a different area from the one you think. You have
the imagination of a dressmaker. Make dresses." Outrage. A few
years later a ladies' fashion department was added to the *Wiener
Werkstätte* and this was the only part of the enterprise to stand on
a sound commercial footing (a phrase to make the artists recoil in
horror) and not be dependent on their patrons, as they so
proudly announced.

But all this artistic individuality constantly going on to new
things has done nothing for our objects of everyday use. There
were no *improvements* in their form and that is all mankind is
interested in. I have kept well away from this vanity fair. People
will say it is just sour grapes, which is true. When I tried to
exhibit a house in Stuttgart it was refused point blank.[2] I had
something that would have been worth showing, namely a
solution for the organization of living rooms in three dimensions,
not two, from one story to the next, as has been the case up to
now. This invention of mine would have saved humanity much
time and labor in its development.[3] But there is no development
in things which have been already solved. They stay in the same
form for centuries until a new invention puts them out of use or
a new cultural form changes them fundamentally.

For the uninitiated who do not understand the aggressive
tone of this article I would just like to explain the difference
between me and other architects. I maintain that it is use which
creates cultural forms, the form of objects, the others that a

newly created form can influence the cultural form (the way we sit, live, eat etc.). Sitting at table while eating, the use of cutlery etc. has not changed for two centuries. Just as fixing and taking out a wood screw has not changed for centuries, so that we have had no change in the form of the screwdriver. We have had the same cutlery for a hundred and fifty years. We have had the same chairs for a hundred and fifty years. And this despite the fact that things all around us have changed, for example carpets instead of sand-strewn floors, because we sit on them; a smooth white ceiling instead one covered in pictures because we don't want to have to look at the ceiling to see our pictures; electric light instead of candles; smooth wood, or, better even, marble, instead rich paneling on our walls — a copy of an old chair (every piece produced by a craftsman is a copy of an object from the past whether it be a month or a hundred years old) fits into any room, as does a Persian rug. It is only fools who need to have their very own cap.

Designing a new dining-room chair seems to me a piece of foolishness, a completely superfluous piece of foolishness, combined with a waste of time and effort. The dining chair of the time of Thomas Chippendale was perfect. It was the solution. It could not be bettered. Like our forks, our sabers, our screwdrivers. People who cannot screw in a screw, people who cannot fence, find it easy to design new screwdrivers, new sabers and new forks. They do it with the help of what they call their artistic imagination. But my saddler says to the artist who brings him a design for a new saddle, "But my dear professor, if I knew as little about horses, about riding, about my work and about leather as you, then I would have your imagination."

The Chippendale chair is so perfect that it will fit into any interior that was produced *after* Chippendale, even into any modern interior of today. However, only the specialist chairmaker can make it. Not the cabinetmaker. But new chairs are produced by cabinetmakers. Both make objects of wood. The bag maker and the saddler both make things out of leather, but a horseman would reject a saddle made by the bag maker. Why?

Because the horseman knows something about riding.

Anyone who can understand chairs that come from the days when people still knew how to sit at the dining table will reject the chairs of today, which are mere shadows of real chairs. They will choose copies of old chairs which not even the cabinetmaker can produce. Since specialist chairmakers are a dying breed, I have often been asked, "What will you do when old Veillich's not around any more?"

He was buried yesterday. Veillich made all my dining chairs. He worked with me faithfully for thirty years. Until the war he had an assistant whose work he held in high regard. He was not particularly well disposed toward people of today. His assistant was killed in the war. After that he worked by himself. He refused to supply poorer quality chairs, and they would have worked out too expensive anyway. Eventually there wasn't even enough work for him alone. My pupils abroad brought him work. In his youth he had worked in Paris. He was deaf, like me, so we got on very well together. The way he went about choosing the wood for every part of the chair! The timber from the lower part of the trunk was used for the back legs and the annual rings had to match the curve exactly. And — no, why should I give away the secrets of a defunct workshop?

He was seventy-seven, it says in the notice of his death. He worked by himself in the big workshop right up until the day he had to take to his bed, slaving away all day, thinking he was making the best chairs for people who could have no idea what treasures they were getting for a mere song. I could not thank my few clients for having commissioned work from me better than by taking them to Veillich. Some day their grandchildren will be grateful to me.

The scene confronting the clients who commissioned work from him was unforgettable: the deaf master craftsman, alone in the great workshop; his faithful wife who passed on every word; married for fifty years, Philemon and Baucis. There were tears in their eyes when they went back out into the street.

I am left with my client's worried question, "What will you

do when he's not there any more?" Since the chairmakers have died out, chairs, wooden chairs, have gone the same way. That is how things die. If they were needed there would be a worthier younger generation to replace them. The successor to the wooden chair will be the Thonet chair which I described as the only modern chair thirty-one years ago. Jeanneret (le Corbusier) realized that too and promoted them in his buildings if, unfortunately, the wrong model. And then wicker chairs. In Paris, in a tailor's *salon*, I have some red-painted wicker chairs. In the dining room of my last house — yes, the one in Starkfriedgasse, Pötzleinsdorf, that terrifies harmless skiers —: Thonet chairs.

But to you, Josef Veillich, master craftsman, I give my thanks. We were both fortunate that our paths crossed. Without me you would have starved and without you I would not have had any chairs, or they would have been at prices I couldn't expect my clients to pay. They would have cost three times what your chairs did. It was the modesty of your needs that made these chairs possible.

While we mourn as we place Josef Veillich's plane in his grave with him, his fellow men, as social beings, and economists will understand why it is the Thonet chair and the wicker chair that have come into dominance.

Notes

1. 1903.
2. The organizers of the exhibition could not agree on the reason for this decision. In Stuttgart they said the burgomaster had something against me personally. Outraged denial by the burgomaster. Then they talked about a lack of space. But at the last moment the architect, Bourgois, had to help out with some designs even though the owner would have liked to have had a house by me. In Frankfurt am Main the chairman of the local branch of the German *Werkbund* said I wasn't nationalistic enough. True, as they understand the term. In those circles my

remark, "Why do the Papuans have a culture and the Germans none?" is seen as anti-German, as a malicious wisecrack. That my remark comes from a bleeding German heart is something the Germans will never understand. (footnote in original)

3. That is the great revolution in architecture: the *spatial* solution of the ground plan. Before Immanuel Kant, mankind could not think spatially and architects were compelled to make the WC as high as the ballroom. The only way they could obtain lower rooms was by dividing in half. Just as mankind will one day play chess in three dimensions, so the other architects will find spatial solutions for the ground plan. (footnote in original)

39. Furniture and People (1929)
Remarks on a craft book

When, as a young boy, I first visited the Austrian Museum —
that is what the museum of applied art is called in Vienna — the
thing that struck me most of all were two massive wood panels,
and they still made an indelible impression on me as an adult.
They were joined in such a way that the color and grain of the
different woods produced an historical picture. The figures were
lifesize and the panels were 360 cm high, one was 373 cm, the
other 376 cm wide. How do I know this? I have taken the
measurements from the bibliographical work by Hans Huth:
*Abraham and David Roentgen and their Neuwied Furniture
Workshop*, (Annual publication for members of the German
Society for Art; with 2 illus. and 120 plates; X. 77pp.) It is
devoted to the workshop which produced these wooden
"tapestries."

This book not only introduces us to the life and work of the
"greatest cabinetmaker of the century," as the encyclopedist,
Baron Grimm, called David Roentgen in a letter of recommenda-
tion to Catherine the Great, we also become acquainted with his
father, Abraham, and the beginnings of their workshop. Abraham, from the Rhineland, worked in Holland, then settled in
London, which was the decisive move of his career. Huth's
works show that when the workshop had been moved to Neuwied by Koblenz engravings from Chippendale's book were
being used. Also, as Huth notes, drawers were made in the
English fashion, with a beading edge, which was not the custom
of German cabinetmakers.

I am delighted to have this book. Throughout my life David
Roentgen has been one of my idols, although all I knew of him
was that he lived and sold Catherine the Great a desk for 20,000
thalers, which she found so ridiculously cheap that she increased
the price. Probably no one has told this story as often and as
insistently as I have. I am convinced that with this kind of recognition craftwork would flourish. But the Catherines seem to have

died out.

And the desk was already finished. It wasn't as if there was a danger of it turning out worse after a previous reduction in price. The next one would have, though! It is a matter of course that if customers voluntarily pay more than the asking price for the products of a workshop these will get better and better. That explains the craftwork principle that the workshop educates its customers. From the book I learned that David Roentgen called himself an English cabinetmaker. The following advertisement appears on p. 28:

David Roentgen, English Cabinet-Maker in Neuwied am Rhein. Manufactures and sells all kinds of furniture and fittings in both the English and the French taste according to the latest styles and invention, to wit desks, chest of drawers, dressing tables, card tables, caskets, work tables and tambours, well-made chairs, canapés etc.

And so on. But where is the most important piece of furniture, the one after which the whole profession is named? Where is the cabinet, the cupboard, the wardrobe or, as they said in those days, the armoire, the chiffonier? The wardrobe is not in the advertisement and, despite the wealth of excellent visual material, it is not illustrated by the author. Is it a conspiracy of silence? No, the object was no longer produced, it was no longer modern. At the time of the Roentgen workshop clothes were not kept in massive wardrobes but in small rooms which the English called "closets." (As in water closet, but that is something quite different.) The French call it a *penderie*, the Germans a *Wandschrank*. The English and French have stuck to this innovation, the Germans have gone back to the way they kept their clothes in the seventeenth century and decorate their rooms with wardrobes, even if they only keep bottled fruit in them. It is up to architects to get rid of the wardrobe. With all due respect to modern ideas in architecture, what is the point if we are still using objects from the time of candle snuffers.

On the contrary! We are more than a hundred years further on. Nowadays we would have to strike out a few more items from Roentgen's list. Today cabinetmakers only make and sell movable pieces of furniture, the rest is part of the house, that is the architect's responsibility. New tenants or owners of an apartment take over everything from their predecessors, either buying or renting it. Today everyone is happy with ceilings, floors, walls and built-in cupboards in the modern style. But the architect should not try to dictate to the craftsman. Furniture that is still made by the cabinetmaker is modern, that by our present-day architects is *not*. If an architect "designs" the furniture then one wonders, "Will all these things go with each other?" Only if they are *modern*, of course. Modern things always go together. Shoes, socks, dresses, shirts, leather suitcases. These must not be designed by an architect because he has no idea what is modern. But in David Roentgen's time there were modern people such as only our engineers and tailors are today. People who want to produce the best things they can, within their limits, without being aware of what is modern. For it is awareness of it that precludes modernity. Here is the sharp dividing line between true human beings and those who just look human. Time separates the wheat from the chaff and only acknowledges the true human being.

With his wooden panels David Roentgen gave me an insight into my own century. I understood at once. It is no longer a matter of furniture, but of walls. Of built-in furniture, we would say. That explains the strong impression made on any unspoiled human being, therefore on every child.

Every person emerges from the womb with modern nerves. Transforming them into nerves that are not modern is what we call education.

As chance would have it, when I was in America I worked in a marquetry factory for a while. At first as assistant draftsman, then at the hot sanding disk, then as cutter (twelve thicknesses were always cut), then as inlayer. It was the thought of these wooden "tapestries" that gave me the strength to learn to love this craft, even though I was trained as a bricklayer, a fact which I consider more important than having studied at the technical university.

But every reader of this book should remember that David Roentgen was part of a great revolution in cabinetmaking, a revolution which lies in the concept of quality. It is quite wrong when people say that such good workmanship is impossible nowadays. The opposite is true. That kind of work is standard in any cabinetmaker's workshop. The late painter of the Künstler-haus in Vienna was certainly correct *as far as craftwork is concerned* when he said, "We'd all like to paint like Raphael or Michelangelo, if we were paid for it."

40. The Vienna City Council's Tenements Cannot Tolerate Criticism (1930)
A conversation with Adolf Loos in Paris

After a long absence the well-known architect, Adolf Loos, who rejects the designation "artist" because he believes the architect should be a craftsman serving people's need for practical and comfortable houses, has returned to Paris, where he has attracted a considerable following. Two years ago he was invited to Czechoslovakia to carry out a large-scale architectural project and serious illness made his stay there longer than expected. But now he has returned, completely recovered, full of new impressions, ideas and plans, and talked in his usual original and witty manner about his profession, his colleagues and his works.

"In the interest of 'modern' architects," *he said among other things,* "I regret the appearance of one particular phenomenon, in Paris as well as elsewhere. The buildings on the place de l'Opéra look much more 'modern' than those recently built, with the sole exception of the bank on boulevard Malesherbes. Only a tiny minority of architects have comprehended that they should be craftsman and not 'artists.' For that reason tailors and shoe-makers have a much more 'modern' approach than they. 'Modern,' you see, is anything that does not attract attention to itself, and is subject only to considerations of practicality and, I should add, decency. In an earlier time my buildings attracted attention for a while, like someone attending a fancy dress ball in white tie and tails, but since then people have become accustomed to the modern style of building, as they have to the gentleman in white tie and tails. Architects must finally see that it is not their place to be artists, but craftsmen, that their task is to work in the service of human needs, as does, say, a cook, while an artist has the right to speak through his 'superfluous' works.

"I will describe two little scenes which seem very character-istic to me. Once I was telling a very well-known colleague that I had seen an apartment for which he had done the interior. 'My friend,' said my colleague, 'that interior is out of date. I did it three years ago.' — 'That answer,' I replied, 'shows the difference between us. I could have told you the interior was no good three years ago, you only see it now.'

"Respect for materials is a fundamental prerequisite for any decent craftsman. A house must remain modern until it collapses. Anyone who produces work according to the fashion of the moment is a swindler who is duping his client.

"The second scene. Once, when I was in a menswear shop with another well-known colleague choosing a tie, I asked him which he considered the least modern. And that was the one I bought, for in that way I was sure I had not bought a tie that would be subject to fashion.

"The great significance people accord to fashion nowadays is a consequence of the proletarization of the world. The aristocrat is conservative in matters of fashion as in all others. He cannot bring himself to put aside, according to the dictates of fashion, the many fine suits, all made to order, he has hanging in his closet, while a man who only has a single off-the-rack suit is quite happy to replace it with a more modern one when it is past its best.

"The latest fashion in Central Europe is metal furniture, something which must seem quite comic to the French since back in the dark ages *le bon roi Dagobert* had a throne made on those principles.

"In recent years I have completely turned away from my homeland. People in Vienna hold that against me. They are also annoyed at the way I have criticized the new tenements built by the city council which have no running hot water, no central heating or bathrooms and to which, anyway, I cannot with the best will in the world give my approval.

"Perhaps they would accept that. The thing to which the Viennese most take objection, I think, is that I prefer French cuisine to theirs. Running down Viennese cuisine is a sin that will never be forgiven me . . ."

41. Adolf Loos on Josef Hoffmann (1931)

When, in 1896, I returned to Vienna after a three-year absence in America and saw my colleagues I could hardly believe my eyes. All these architects were dressed like "artists." Not like other people but — to American eyes — like clowns. They had a specially trained tailor who constructed these costumes from magnificent materials. People laughed, but the government, on the advice of journalists, gave them all doctorates and professorships. I was for good old Viennese cabinetmaking, tradition and quality; their work looked like their dress. I was excluded from their circle. I was, as my clothes demonstrated, no artist. I had a regular subscription with the Goldman and Salatsch menswear store and advised my colleagues to give up their fripperies and do the same. The response was pitying smiles. Then I received a commission to do an interior. I invited Josef Hoffmann and Kolo Moser to see it. We went in a cab on a Wednesday afternoon. The Stößler apartment. The two of them looked at the unusual things in silence. Then we parted. Two days later I was in Goldman and Salatsch's and the old gentleman said, "I think, Herr Loos, we have you to thank for a new customer." I had told everyone, artists and writers, to go to Goldman and Salatsch so I had no idea who it might be. "Who is it?" — "A professor from the School of Applied Art, he's called Josef Hoffmann." You could have knocked me down with a feather. "Since when has he been a customer?" — "Since the day before yesterday, in the afternoon." — "What time did he come?" — "Have a look in the customer ledger, Johann. When was Professor Hoffmann here?" — "At 4:30 in the afternoon." Fifteen minutes after he left me.

Since that day — the firm of Goldman and Salatsch can presumably supply the exact date — Josef Hoffmann has been dressed in the European style. And the straight line became the characteristic feature of the *Sezession*! They sat in upholstered boxes, they made silver cubes and called them teapots until I was finally released from this misunderstanding of my doctrine by the appearance of Dagobert Peche, whom they proceeded to imitate next.

The misunderstanding of my doctrine was taken over by the Weimar Bauhaus. It was called "New Objectivity." And now, finally, Josef Hoffmann has adopted this "New Objectivity." So to all the evils since 1896 even more complicated forms of ornamentation have been added: needless constructions, orgies of the preferred materials (concrete, glass, iron). Bauhaus and constructivist romanticism is no better than the romanticism of ornament.

The day must come when all these gentlemen will get together to stop working according to slogans and, as I wanted in 1896 when I helped Josef Hoffmann to dress like a civilized European, work in the *modern* manner.

42. Project to Save a Pine Wood[1] (1931)

There is a plot of ground on the avenue du Littoral at Juan-les-Pins 46 meters long, covered by a pine wood. The part bordering the avenue to a depth of 24 meters has been released for building. To get the maximum out of the plot a hotel is to be built. An existing project proposes destroying a third of this woodland in order to make room for a horseshoe-shaped building.

I, on the other hand, propose a project which would allow the whole length of the woodland to be saved by removing the two wings and making the building high enough to recoup the floor space lost. A large arch running a third of the length will allow the woodland to be seen. The restaurant and dance floor, constructed with a terrace, will be high enough to allow a view of Cap d'Antibes and Cannes, which will make it an attraction for the whole stretch of coast. The ground plan itself is not a new idea, but is conceived after the system that has already been tried and tested in the Palais Wilson at Juan-les-Pins. However, the street level is given over to stores, the restaurant is on the next-to-top floor and the dance floor on the terrace. A new system of ventilation is planned for the kitchenettes and bathrooms of the apartments.

Notes

1. Original in French

PLACE AND DATE OF THE FIRST PUBLICATION OF
THE ESSAYS IN THIS VOLUME:

A Competition Organized by the City of Vienna.
Eine Konkurrenz der Stadt Wien. *Die Zeit*, Vienna, Nov. 6, 1897.

From Otto Wagner's Class.
Aus der Wagner-Schule. *Neue Freie Presse*, Vienna, July 31, 1898.

A Viennese Architect.
Ein Wiener Architekt. *Dekorative Kunst*, Munich, vol. II, no. 11,
    1898.

The Potemkin City.
Die Potemkin'sche Stadt. *Ver Sacrum*, Vienna, no. 7, July 1898.

To Our Young Architects.
Unseren jungen Architekten. *Ver Sacrum*, Vienna, no. 7, July
    1898.

The Old and the New Style in Architecture.
Die alte und die neue Richtung. *Der Architekt*, Vienna, in der
    Baukunst vol. IV, 1898.

Building Materials.
Die Baumaterialien. *Neue Freie Presse*, Vienna, Aug. 28, 1898.

The Principle of Cladding.
Das Princip der Bekleidung. *Neue Freie Presse*, Vienna, Sept. 4,
    1898.

The Story of the Poor Little Rich Man.
Vom armen reichen Mann. *Neues Wiener Tagblatt*, Vienna, April
    26, 1900.

Guided Tours of Apartments.
Wohnungswanderungen. Privately printed, 1907.

The Discovery of Vienna.
Die Entdeckung Wiens. *Fremden-Blatt*, Vienna, April 7, 1907.

An Appeal to the Citizens of Vienna.
Aufruf an die Wiener. *Die Fackel*, Vienna, April 9, 1910.

Some Questions Regarding Viennese Architecture.
Wiener Architekturfragen. *Reichspost*, Vienna, Oct. 1, 1910.

My First Building!
Mein erstes Haus! *Der Morgen*, Vienna, Oct. 3, 1910.

Architecture.
Architektur. Excerpt printed with the title "Ueber Architektur"
in *Der Sturm*, Berlin, Dec. 15, 1910.

Otto Wagner. *Reichspost*, Vienna, July 13, 1911.

My Building on Michaelerplatz.
Mein Haus am Michaelerplatz 12. Lecture, Vienna, Dec. 11, 1911.

The Mystery of Acoustics.
Das Mysterium der Akustik. *Der Merkur*, Vienna, vol. 1, Jan.
1912.

Heimatkunst. Lecture, Vienna, Nov. 20, 1912.

My School of Building.
Meine Bauschule. *Der Architekt*, Vienna, vol. 10, Oct. 1913.

Rules for Building in the Mountains.
Regeln für den, der in den Bergen baut. *Jahrbuch der Schwarzwald'schen Schulanstalten*, Vienna, 1913.

Adolf Loos on Viennese Buildings.
Adolf Loos über Wiener Gebäude.

Winter Sports Hotel on the Semmering.
Wintersporthotel am Semmering.

The Hotel on Friedrichstraße in Vienna.
Hotel Friedrichstraße in Wien.

Architecture and the Cafe.
Architektur und Caféhaus. Notes by a participant in the seminar, 1913/14.

The Opening of the Technical Museum.
Eröffnung des Technischen Museums. *Neues 8 Uhr-Blatt*, Vienna, May 2, 1918.

Guidelines for a Regulatory Body for the Arts.
Richtlinien für ein Kunstamt. *Der Friede*, Vienna, March 29, 1919.

Art and Architecture.
Art et Architecture. *Action — Cahiers individualistes de Philosophie et d'Art*, Paris, Oct. 1920.

Rules for Social Housing Developments.
Regeln für die Siedlung. Manuscript, 1920.

The House with One Wall.
Das Haus mit einer Mauer. Submission for a patent, Feb. 11, 1921.

Houses for the Lainz Social Housing Development.
Siedlungshäuser Lainz. Privately printed, July 22, 1921.

Social Housing Development Day.
Der Tag der Siedler. *Neue Freie Presse*, Vienna, April 3, 1921.

Learning a New Way of Living!
Wohnen lernen! *Neues Wiener Tagblatt*, May 15, 1921.

The Chicago Tribune Column. *Zeitschrift der Österr. Ingenieur-und Architektenvereins*, Vienna, no. 3/4, Jan. 26, 1923.

Grand Babylon Hotel.
Das Grand-Hotel Babylon. *Die Neue Wirtschaft*, Vienna, Feb. 14, 1924.

Furnishing a Modern Apartment.
Die Einrichtung der modernen Wohnung. *Die Neue Wirtschaft*, Vienna, Feb. 14, 1924.

On Thrift.
Von der Sparsamkeit. *Wohnungskultur*, Brno, no. 2/3, 1924.

Josef Veillich. *Frankfurter Zeitung*, Aug. 25, 1929.

Furniture and People.
Möbel und Menschen. *Frankfurter Zeitung*, Aug. 28, 1929.

The Vienna City Council's Tenements Cannot Tolerate Criticism.
Die Wiener Gemeindebauten vertragen keine Kritik.Conversation with Adolf Loos in Paris, 1930.

Adolf Loos on Josef Hoffmann.
Adolf Loos über Josef Hoffmann. *Das neue Frankfurt*, no. 2, Feb. 1921.

Project to Save a Pine Wood.
Projet de Sauvetage d'une Pinède. *L'Architecture d'aujourd'hui*, Paris, Oct. 1931.

ILLUSTRATIONS

illustration p. 94: Building on Michaelerplatz: plans submitted with planning application.

illustration p. 128: Hotel on Friedrichstraße, Vienna. Façade.

illustration, p. 145: "House with One Wall" method of construction.

illustration p. 148: Projects for Row houses in Housing Developments. Ground plans, section and elevation of the street frontage of a 6-meter type (scale 1: 300).
Planned using the "house with one wall" construction method: the party walls alone bear both the joists, which run parallel to the street frontage, and the front and rear walls of the house which are simply hung between each pair of load-bearing walls.

illustration p. 151: *Houses for a Social Housing Development (Project 1921)*
— *longitudinal section*
— *upper-floor ground plan*
— *lower-floor ground plan.*

illustration p. 153: *Project for Row Houses for Housing Project, 1920-1922. Corner type, ground plan (scale 1: 150); viewed from living room/kitchen, joists laid from party wall to party wall.*
[words on plan, from top to bottom and left to right: yard; veranda; larder; toilet; scullery; entrance; vestibule; stove; stairs up; kitchen/living room].

illustration p. 169: [handwriting] Why once again (as so often in other matters) I have been pestering the most charming diplomat in Vienna — Adolf Loos — Vienna, Oct. 19, 1922.
Competition entry for a palatial newspaper building for the Chicago Tribune, *1922.*
Dedication to Legationsrat Dr. Peterka.
Werner J. Schweiger Archive, Vienna.
illustrations pp. 173 and 198 have no accompanying text.

Also available from Ariadne Press

Adolf Loos

Ornament and Crime
Selected Essays

Selected and with an Introduction
by Adolf Opel
Translated by Michael Mitchell

ISBN 1-57241-046-9; 204 pages